THE GOSPEL ACCORDING TO PONTIVS PILATE

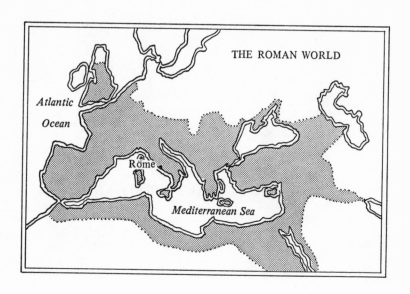

THE ROMAN WORLD

Atlantic
Ocean

Rome

Mediterranean Sea

JAMES R. MILLS

THE GOSPEL ACCORDING TO PONTIVS PILATE

SAN FRANCISCO BOOK COMPANY

San Francisco 1977

Library of Congress Cataloging in Publication Data

Mills, James R   1927–
    The Gospel according to Pontius Pilate.
    1. Pilate, Pontius, 1st cent.—Fiction.   2.   Jesus Christ
        —Fiction.   I.   Title.
PZ4.M65573Go   [PS3563.I42315]   813'.5'4   77-4576
                    ISBN 0-913374-77-6

            10 9 8 7 6 5 4 3 2 1

Printed in the United States of America

Contents

Preface

The time has arrived in my life when I, Pontius Pilate, can say with Julius Caesar, "I have lived long enough, whether for fame or fortune." Often in recent years I have found myself reflecting back upon the past, as old men do for lack of other pleasures, and it has become apparent that one action of mine, which seemed routine enough at the time, was a matter of some importance. I refer to my ordering of the execution of the Galilean carpenter and visionary, Jesus of Nazareth, now often called Jesus Christ, while I was governor of Judea, Samaria, and Idumea.

I would never have believed it then if I had been told that there would be controversy about the fellow thirty years later. In the last few months interest has risen to a level higher than ever before, since the destruction of Rome by fire, and the official conclusion that the Christians were responsible for the holocaust. Now that so many of them are being crucified there in the arena, lighted by others being burned as torches, they have become a chief topic for discussion in the ruined city, I am given to understand.

The few old friends who visit me here in exile generally ask me to tell them something about that strange carpenter. So I have told the story from time to time. The growing interest in the subject has moved me to undertake the task of setting it down on paper.

Perhaps I should acknowledge in passing that there are people who say that those wretched Christians are not guilty of the crime for which they now are being punished. They say it is not in accordance with Christian principles to have caused so much death and destruction. Be that as it may, scandal mongers spreading the rumor that the Emperor himself was responsible for burning the city made it desirable to assign blame for the great fire promptly and to proceed at once with punishments. Whether persons punished are actually guilty of the crimes with which they are charged is not the only factor to be taken into account sometimes. That can be an uncomfortable truth, as it was for me in the case of the carpenter himself.

But it seems that the Emperor wants to be rid of the Christians in any case. They are subversive of the interests of the state in their attempts to divert the Roman populace from belief in the official gods of Rome, including the Emperor Nero himself, whose divinity is important to him, and to the state. Besides which, they are the objects of popular fear and loathing, because of the stories about them drinking blood as a part of their rituals.

What I shall try to do is relate and explain the events in the life of Jesus of Nazareth, to let the reader know how the man was seen during his lifetime by the world in general. I shall point out those peculiarities that set him apart from others among the collection of fakers, zealots, and magicians who have recently claimed to be the messiah, or deliverer, of the Jews. Some of them have attracted substantial followings. However, with the exception of this one man, the death of each has resulted in the scattering of his disciples.

I'll give just two examples. When Felix was Procurator of Judea he had to deal with an Egyptian Jew who proclaimed that he would bring down the walls of Jerusalem with the breath of his mouth. This fellow presented himself on the Mount of Olives just to the east of Jerusalem, where the messiah is expected to appear. He assembled four thousand gullible Jews there to attack the city. Felix sent troops and took him prisoner. After the man was executed his movement vanished. Later, while Fadus was Governor, a magician of some skill, named Theudas, persuaded a multitude of people to follow him down to the Jordan River, which he said would divide and allow them to pass through dry-shod. Fadus sent a detachment of cavalry against them which killed a number and took many prisoners. As for Theudas, the soldiers crucified him, cut off his head, and took it to Jerusalem. His following, too, dispersed at once.

What is surprising is the fact that the same falling away has not taken place among the disciples of Jesus Christ, even though the measures being taken to deal with them are thorough and systematic. Not long ago I heard that among those crucified in the arena was the leader of the Christians in Rome, a Galilean fisherman named Peter, who had great authority among them because he had been very close to the carpenter during his lifetime. I have also heard word that another leading apostle of Jesus named Paul was recently beheaded in Rome, but there seems to be some question about it. One thing is sure, if he hasn't been disposed of, he soon will be.

It appears that this particular sect is destined to disappear now and forever in Rome with the death of its leaders and the general slaughter of its members. At most it will persist for a while as just another clandestine mystery cult in some parts of the East. Yet there are lessons to be learned from it.

To understand how Jesus of Nazareth assembled a following that has clung to his memory in the face of adversity during the years since his death, it is necessary to know what went into the making of the legends that surround him.

I remember how it all developed very well. I recall how I read with some interest the first reports received from Galilee about that uncommon man and the stir he occasioned. Actually, we didn't gather a great deal of information about him as long as he remained in Galilee, out of my jurisdiction. I pieced together an account of the early months of his brief career after his death.

Information about the last few months of his life came into my hands as the events took place. When he appeared in Judea, my agents had to put together intelligence reports about him as one of the potential nationalist leaders within my territory. The more his following developed the more my interest grew, until at last he stood before me on the day of his death.

I remained as governor of Judea for half a dozen years after that day. During that time Christianity began to become an influence among the Jews. I set some of my men collecting information about the dead man and his followers. When I was recalled to Rome for trial, I brought copies of that material with me, along with other information bearing upon issues that might have been raised relative to my performance in office. Since then I have added items that have come my way on the subject. Particularly interesting is a collection of sayings of Jesus compiled by certain Christians, which fell into my hands recently.

Because of the part I played in the drama, people with knowledge of the carpenter and his followers have tended to pass it along to me. I have been receiving new information periodically since then about the man himself and the doctrines and activities of the cult, and that has kept old memories from fading.

Because of this, and because I informed myself about their beliefs and customs when I went to govern the Jews, as a governor must do to rule any people well, I am in a position to present the story of the life of Jesus of Nazareth and make understandable what took place and why it did. It is a useful case study in the art of politics.

I am writing for the rulers of this and future generations, and for those who pass judgment upon them, to offer a commentary upon what are the valid tests of truth in government. The world does not change. Political questions are all the same. Only the particulars differ.

Introduction

After Caligula banished me to Gaul thirty-seven years ago, I decided to occupy myself by writing a history of Palestine, in order that Roman policy in respect to the Jews might be better informed. Before I had gotten far with the project new ventures engaged my attention, and I laid it aside. The chapters I completed have remained undisturbed on their roll since that time.

It now occurs to me that parts of that manuscript dealing with the religion and some of the history of the Jews would be useful background for understanding the story of the life and death of Jesus of Nazareth. Therefore, I am offering some of that work of long ago here.

The Jews

Every Roman knows something about the Jews from personal observation. No people is more widely scattered throughout the Empire. They are to be found in every port city on the Mediterranean Sea, living in their own quarters of each town, observing their own odd customs and worshipping their one strange god in their curious temples, or, to use their own term, synagogues. They have only one true temple. That is their national shrine at Jerusalem where hecatombs of dumb beasts are slain daily, in order to wash away the sins of the people with their blood.

It seems to me the antipathy that exists commonly toward the Jews today is based upon their religious insularity. Greeks, Romans, Egyptians, and most other peoples show respect for each others' gods, if only as a matter of courtesy, and even adopt those foreign deities who appeal to them. Romans are willing to pay the god of the Jews due deference; but unlike other nations, the Jews treat our gods with contempt, refusing even to give them the honor a decent respect for our feelings demands. Also, the consistent Jewish refusal to acknowledge the divinity of the emperor has caused them to be looked upon as subjects of questionable loyalty ever since Caesar Augustus was recognized as a god almost a century ago.

The Jews in turn are sensitive about the attitude of Romans and Greeks that the Jewish religion is a barbaric superstition. They are further offended by the misconceptions about their faith that are current among us.

We all know that they believe in one god, and in that we are correct. However, the widely held belief that the god they worship is Bacchus is erroneous, unfortunately. That mistake arises from a misunderstanding of the meaning of a famous golden grapevine which adorns the temple in Jerusalem. There are also certain rituals at their Feast of Tabernacles which have led people into this error.

In Rome I have heard it said that their unwillingness to eat the flesh of swine stems from their paying divine honors to that animal. That, too, is untrue.

Apion, the grammarian, said that the Jews offer a Greek in sacrifice every year and eat his entrails in a religious ceremony; and that they worship an ass's head. This is the purest of fantasy. Although I do dislike them myself, I think no good comes from wild fears based on misunderstandings. It should be enough to hate people for what they are, rather than for what they are not.

Their god is a mysterious god. They believe him to be invisible and omnipotent, the creator of the world and the father of mankind. They believe he is present on earth in the most holy part of their great temple in Jerusalem, a dark chamber in which no one but the high priest may set foot, and he only on the most holy day of the year. Pompey found it to be an empty room when he entered it by right of conquest. Everyone was astonished to hear there was no god to be seen and worshipped in that tremendous edifice.

One of the things generally known about the Jews is that they believe their god selected them to be his chosen people, an opinion unshaken by a history filled with misfortune. This belief is construed by most people to mean only that the Jews hold the opinion that they are better than the rest of us, which they do. Yet that feeling alone is no different from the good opinion every nation has of itself.

With those self-conscious Jews, however, being the chosen people of god is not so much an honor as it is a burden laid upon them. In a typical passage upon the subject from Moses, their great lawgiver, he reports their god as promising, "If you will obey my voice and keep my covenant, then you shall be a treasure to me above all peoples . . . . And you shall be unto me a kingdom of priests and a holy nation." Elsewhere their god is represented as saying, "I give thee for a light to the gentiles."

(The term gentile is used by them to cover all of us who are not Jews.)

A central concept of their religion is the coming of an age when all mankind will live as brothers, as one family under the rule of their god as father. They believe they were selected to receive the law through Moses so that they could, by observing it, set an example for all nations. They are sure their god's chief concern is that they comply with the commandments that they believe he gave to them. To the extent that they fall short, the golden age is delayed for all the world.

Their view of their role in the cosmos is grandiose but benevolent. They are troubled by the fact that their Roman rulers smile at such presumption on the part of an insignificant people. Romans have always liked Quintus Ennius for saying, "The gods don't care what men do; if they did, things would go well with good men and ill with bad ones, which is seldom the case."

Usually religious men are so caught up in their prayers and religious disputes that they don't take time to notice the world as it is. Perhaps they cannot stand to think about it.

Another feature of their religion involves their relationship to the land of Palestine. According to Moses, their god promised it to Israel as their home. It is curious how they can convince themselves that their god thinks so much of them. A god who was fond of them should have promised them something better. Nevertheless, it is believed by them to be contrary to the will of their god that any gentile should possess any part of Palestine. Their law forbids them to sell or even rent a plot of land to any non-Jew.

Their religion is based upon five books attributed to Moses, known as the *Torah*, as well as the writings of other prophets of ancient times. Most of those authorities

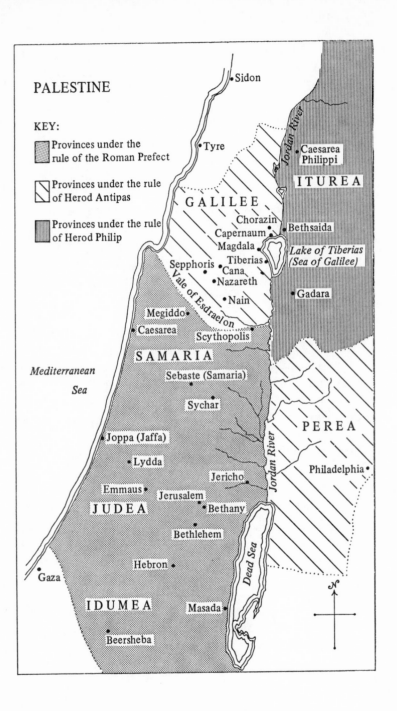

PALESTINE

KEY:

Provinces under the rule of the Roman Prefect

Provinces under the rule of Herod Antipas

Provinces under the rule of Herod Philip

• Sidon

• Tyre

Jordan River

• Caesarea Philippi

ITUREA

GALILEE

Chorazin
Capernaum •
• Bethsaida
Magdala •
Lake of Tiberias
(Sea of Galilee)
Sepphoris • Tiberias
• Cana
• Nazareth
• Nain
• Gadara

Vale of Esdraelon

Megiddo •
• Caesarea
Scythopolis

SAMARIA

Mediterranean
Sea

• Sebaste (Samaria)

• Sychar

PEREA

• Joppa (Jaffa)

Jordan River

• Lydda

• Philadelphia

Jericho •
Emmaus •
Jerusalem
• Bethany
JUDEA
• Bethlehem

Dead Sea

Hebron •

• Gaza

IDUMEA

• Masada

N

• Beersheba

make reference to a savior of the Jewish people. In Hebrew he is called *the messiah*, which means *the anointed one*. In Greek the word *messiah* becomes *Christ*. He is to come and deliver them from oppression and reign as king in Jerusalem, not only over the Jews but over all other peoples in an empire which will be eternal and world-wide.

Most of the messianic legends call up memories of King David, their greatest ruler, who ruled over all of Palestine and much of Syria. The death of his son Solomon marked the end of the great age of the Jewish nation. Ever since then the Jews have been yearning for its return. The messiah is to be the descendant of David who will restore the glory of the old king's dynasty to the descendents of Israel. They often pray for his early appearance.

Originally there were twelve tribes of Jews. After the death of Solomon, civil war divided them into a southern kingdom of two tribes and a northern one of ten.

Because the northern ten tribes were troublesome subjects in the Assyrian Empire almost seven hundred years ago, Sargon II dispersed them throughout his empire. A few were allowed to remain in the territory of the northern kingdom, which includes the land now called Samaria. They intermarried with the Assyrians and other peoples who had been resettled on the lands which had been vacated. By reason of their mixed ancestry, the Samaritans have been looked down upon by the Jews ever since. I was surprised to learn that Jews are not permitted to eat food prepared by the hands of a Samaritan. The fact that a Samaritan touched it makes it unclean.

About a hundred years after the demise of the northern kingdom, the southern kingdom was conquered by Nebuchadnezzar of Babylon, and its leaders were carried off into captivity in Babylonia. Later they were allowed to return to their homeland, and many did so. Conflicts with the Samaritans over the rebuilding of Jerusalem and the restoration of the Temple caused further hostility to develop between the two peoples.

At that time the Samaritan king declared Mount Gerizim in Samaria to be more holy then the Temple Mount in Jerusalem, and the Samaritans built their own temple there. The result is that today the word Samaritan is used to mean *heretic* among Jews.

Since their repatriation to Palestine the Jews have been tributaries to the Persian, Macedonian, Egyptian, Seleucid, and Roman Empires, with only occasional interludes of independence. The last few centuries have been a time of turmoil and tribulation to them, a time of punishment. They see their subjugation as evidence of their god's disfavor.

Recent History of the Jewish Nation

The forces at work in modern Palestine generally date from the time of the conquests of Alexander the Great. He established Greek military colonies in the land. Entire Jewish cities were presented to veterans of his armies, who brought their families with them to take over the homes and property of the Jews who had been driven out.

These cities were given Hellenic names and soon became as Greek as Athens itself. The citizens of a city like Gadara or Scythopolis, for the most part Epicureans or Stoics, were inclined to find in the severe faith of the Jews a source of amusement. There soon developed among the wealthier Jews a party of intellectuals who were in tune with Greek culture and Greek customs, for whose company my wife and I were often thankful during our years there.

Most Jews, however, resented the intrusion of aliens, whose sophistication they looked upon as depravity, as much as they detested the rule of a foreign monarch. Two centuries ago Antiochus Epiphanes IV, the Seleucid emperor of Syria, decided to impose a permanent solution to the problem presented by the Jews. He saw that it was their religion which made them different from other peoples and difficult to govern, so he undertook to put an end to it. He forbade various Jewish rites, especially circumcision and the observance of the sabbath day, and commanded his soldiers to execute anyone who disobeyed.

In the Temple in Jerusalem he erected a colossal statue of the Olympian Zeus, whose head represented his own. To further profane their most holy place, Antiochus ordered the sacrifice of hogs upon the altar. Adding a final turn of the screw, he ordered that the Jewish priests eat the flesh of the dead swine on penalty of death. If he had lived among the Jews as I did, he could have anticipated the result. The priests chose death and became martyr heroes of the revolution that flared up.

Under the leadership of a family of warrior priests called the Maccabees, the Jews defied the power of the Seleucid Empire. After twenty-five years of bitter civil war, they gained their independence.

Judas, the greatest hero among the Maccabees, re-established the theocratic form of government when he accepted the office of high priest on a hereditary basis. Before long a successor assumed the title of king. This new royal family became known as the Hasmonean dynasty. The classes of citizens and the political parties which exist today were taking form during those years.

Surviving from ancient times was the hereditary priesthood. It had become the aristocracy and the ruling class in Judea. Until recently only its members could serve on the Great Sanhedrin, the supreme court of the Jews which had wide jurisdiction at the time.

There grew up around the priestly class a political party known as the Sadducees. Originally they were organized as partisans of King John Hyrcanus to support a policy of conquest which was objectionable to a great number of religious Jews. The materialism inherent in such a program seemed inconsistent with what should be the ideals of a state ruled by a king who was also the high priest of such a god.

The Sadducees were the high officials in the government of John Hyrcanus. They supported his policy of accommodation with foreign powers, especially the Roman republic. This attitude toward Rome has remained a basic principle among the Sadducees ever since.

Today they are still the priests and judges by right of inheritance, but they are declining in influence. As judges they adhere to the policies of the Pharisees, who are the majority party, otherwise the people would not put up with them.

Insofar as their religious doctrines are concerned, Sadducees only believe in the ancient written law of Moses. They are distinguished from the other Jews in that they believe there is no life after death, because Moses did not refer to it.

While the Sadducees are the party of the priests, the Pharisees are the party supported by the majority of the scribes. They are a growing class of scholars who study and explain the law of their god, a function once performed by the priests but relinquished by them as the increasing legalistic tendencies in the Jewish religion developed. The title *rabbi* is applied to those who teach.

Unlike the Sadducees, the Pharisees believe in a life beyond the grave. They hold that the wicked will be punished then for their transgressions on earth, but that the virtuous shall rise to live again in eternal bliss.

The name *Pharisee* is derived from the Hebrew word

separated, because they separated themselves from those who were not also Pharisees. They are strict in their observation of the Jewish law and precise in its definition. They believe in a continuing development of interpretation of the law. Interpretations become binding by a vote of an assembly of accredited teachers. This constant evolution of the law has made it more and more complex. It is one of the eternal unchanging truths that any code of laws which may be amended by lawyers will become ever more complicated until no one can understand it but lawyers, and they will disagree.

That is why the Pharisees will not eat in the homes of those who are not Pharisees. They are afraid of becoming defiled by eating with men less well-informed about the requirements of ritual cleanliness. So I never ate with any of them in all my time there. By all accounts, I didn't miss much.

The Pharisees are the spokesmen for the majority of Jews in matters of religion, although there are only about six thousand of them. They follow no particular professions, and may be carpenters, merchants, farmers, scribes, or anything else. Under ordinary circumstances they are not really a political party. They take little interest in government unless it impinges upon their religious practices.

Today the Sadducees still retain technical control of the religion of the country, because they still constitute a majority of the membership of the Great Sanhedrin. However, the Pharisees have been admitted to membership since well before my time in Palestine.

There is also a party called the Essenes, a monastic order so separated from society that it plays practically no role in public affairs. While the Essenes have some interesting peculiarities, they are of little political importance. I shall not take the time to describe them here.

The old order died with the Hasmonean dynasty when Herod the Great seized the throne, during the eighth year of the second triumvirate.

The story of his rise to power is a remarkable tale of ability, ambition, and guile on the part of three generations. His grandfather was a clever Arab chieftain who rose in the government of the Hasmoneans to a high rank.

The last undisputed monarch of the Hasmonean line was a queen named Alexandra. When she died she left her crown to her son Hyrcanus II. Another son named Aristobolus deposed him. Herod's father, whose name was Antipater, aroused Hyrcanus to stand up for his rights, and civil war broke out.

Both princes appealed for support to Pompey the Great, who was then campaigning triumphantly throughout the East. Pompey sided with Hyrcanus, but deprived him of the throne, leaving him only the office of high priest. The rule of the country was delivered to Antipater, and his sons Herod and Phasael, who had ingratiated themselves with Pompey.

Antipater gained a name for foresight when he allied himself with Rome, as then personified by Pompey. He confirmed that reputation by making himself valuable to Julius Caesar when the fortunes of war ran against Pompey. The good judgment of Antipater earned him the appointment from Caesar as Procurator of Judea. In that position he was able to secure for Herod the post of Governor of Galilee.

When the civil war broke out following the assassination of Caesar, and Cassius seized control of the East, Antipater, Phasael, and Herod survived by serving Cassius collecting money to finance the war. Antipater was poisoned at that time by an enemy and Herod took his place.

After the defeat of Brutus and Cassius at Philippi, Herod appealed to Antony, on the grounds that Cassius had given him no choice but to serve him. As fortune would have it, Herod and Antony had been close friends when they both were brave young soldiers serving Julius Caesar in Egypt. Antony was always a practical man as well as one who valued old friendships, so he granted Herod his father's position and powers.

Soon after that the Parthians invaded Judea, killed Phasael, and placed Antigonus, the son of Aristobolus, on the throne. Herod narrowly escaped with his life. When he appeared in Rome as an exile, Mark Antony presented him to the Senate and recounted his past service to Rome. Having secured the support of Octavian, Antony moved that Herod be declared King of the Jews. After the motion carried, the new king left the Senate on the arms of Antony and Octavian, to a great banquet Antony gave in his honor, having gained a kingdom and a place in history.

When he returned to Palestine, it was with the legions of Sosius, the Governor of Syria, who had orders to implement the act of the Senate making Herod the king. After a bloody siege of Jerusalem, Herod was seated upon the throne. Antigonus was beheaded in Antioch, by order of Antony, ending the last hope for restoration of Hasmonean rule.

During the early years of his reign, Herod the Great had difficulty hanging onto his crown, to say nothing of his head. After Cleopatra gained ascendancy over Antony, her most immediate political aim was to acquire Palestine as an Egyptian province. Herod had once showed better judgment than Antony or Caesar by rejecting her advances, and like any woman she remembered it. By deft maneuvering, Herod swayed Antony, and Cleopatra was able to coax only a few of his provinces out of her new husband before they both lost everything to Octavian and Marcus Agrippa at the battle of Actium.

The greatest triumph of King Herod occurred after Actium. When other allies of Antony were fleeing for their lives to the ends of the earth, he went to Crete and appeared before the victorious Octavian, soon to be Caesar Augustus, saying truthfully that he had been a faithful friend to Antony through every peril. He said he wanted to be just as loyal a friend to Caesar. To the surprise of everyone, he was accepted as such. By all accounts he was a very charming man when he chose to be. In time it was said that Herod was Caesar's best friend, excepting only his son-in-law, the great Marcus Agrippa. It was also said that Herod was Agrippa's best friend, excepting only Caesar.

Among his problems as king was the fact that he had no legitimate claim to the throne. He was resented as a usurper and as a foreigner because he was an Arab, of the nation of the Idumeans or Edomites. This tribe had been conquered by King John Hyrcanus I, and forced to convert to Judaism. At that time they were officially declared to be Jews, but they were, according to Jewish scriptures, descended from a man named Esau, the brother of the patriarch Jacob, from who the Jews are descended. Jacob is supposed to have done Esau and his descendants out of their birthright as their god's chosen people through some rather sharp dealing. The result, according to the story, was that the Edomites were condemned to be the servants of the Jews. They called Herod the *Edomite Servant* because of his relationship to Caesar. Yet he earned the title *Herod the Great* by his success in overcoming all of his enemies and in extending his rule over most of the land of Palestine. He added to his reputation by his remarkable program of building and rebuilding cities. Some of the finest towns in the entire world are the Greek cities he built in his kingdom, like the present capital city Caesarea, which he constructed on the site of the ancient Mediterranean port city of Strato's Tower. Rivaling his works in Palestine are the beautifications of cities in Syria and Greece he undertook as gestures of majestic goodwill. He erected temples to Roman gods in the gentile cities of his kingdom, which was considered by Jews to be horrifying impiety on his part. He also beautified those cities with many fine buildings, colonnades, and so forth. However, he could not do such elaborate works in the Jewish cities of Palestine because the law of Moses does not tolerate extensive decorations, and the Pharisees insisted upon the observance of that law.

To try to win the loyalty of the Jews he undertook to reconstruct and beautify their ancient Temple in Jerusalem. The Jews are very proud of it. It is a common saying among them that anyone who has not seen Herod's building has not seen anything beautiful. Yet it did not reduce the animosity of the public toward him. They resented the taxes necessary to pay for the king's projects.

In any event, Herod had never been forgiven by the Jews for calling upon Rome to conquer them on his behalf. The horrors of the bloody siege of Jerusalem were fresh in their memories.

Nor had they forgiven him for ordering the execution of the majority of their supreme court, the Great Sanhedrin, shortly after the conquest of Jerusalem, to bring it under his control. Herod was settling an old score when he did that. The Sanhedrin had once attempted to try him for murder, when, as Governor of Galilee, he had executed without trial a Jewish zealot named Hezekiah, who had raised a rebellion. Called before the

Sanhedrin, Herod brought soldiers with him and defied it. When those old enemies were delivered into his hand, he snuffed them out. The Great Sanhedrin is made up of the highest religious officials. Herod's slaughter of these judges engendered a bitter antipathy toward him on the part of all religious Jews.

It still rankled in the minds of his people that Herod had offered a formal sacrifice to Jupiter after the Senate had declared him to be the King of the Jews. No subsequent expression of devotion to the god of the Jews could entirely erase the memory of Herod piously walking in a ceremonial procession with Antony, following the sacrificial bull, which had been bedecked with the usual garlands of flowers, as it was led to the Temple of Jupiter on the Capitoline Hill. The Jewish community in Rome reported the gala event with awful shame to the Jews of Palestine.

King Herod offended his people in things both large and small. Although Greeks were looked upon as foreigners who had no proper place in the promised land, Herod surrounded himself with Greek intellectuals as friends and advisers. His government was carried on by men of Greek culture.

He supported Greek athletic activities, and gave liberal grants to the old games at Olympia. Finally, in recognition of his contributions he was made honorary president of the Olympic Games. In Judea he built stadiums, gymnasiums, and hippodromes, even in the holy city of Jerusalem itself, to the chagrin of the Pharisees. The games were celebrated every four years in Caesarea and Jerusalem. Religious Jews were shocked by the nudity in Greek athletic contests because of the prohibitions against nakedness in their scriptures.

For these reasons and for others the king was hated by his subjects. To maintain his control over them he depended on foreign mercenary soldiers, Germans, Thracians, and Gauls. To keep the Jews from revolt he built mighty fortresses at strategic points. In his early years he erected one in Jerusalem itself, where its towers overshadow the courts of the Temple. He called it the *Antonia* in honor of his best friend at the time, Mark Antony. It dominates the city, representing the power of Rome.

There was turmoil in the palace for years because of intrigues within the royal family. Herod's children and other relatives plotted constantly against each other. He married a beautiful Hasmonean princess named Mariamme to try to assure the succession of the crown for his descendants. Ultimately he killed her, as well as her grandfather, the former King Hyrcanus II, in addition to her mother and her brother. Later he ordered the deaths of her two sons by him. He loved her more than any of his other nine wives, yet he executed her on the basis of unproven accusations from other ambitious relatives. The same was the fate of her sons, whom he had chosen to succeed him. The conspiracies within his household never ceased. He was killing members of his tumultuous family almost until the day he died. It was enough to madden a saint, and King Herod at his best had been passionate, harsh, and suspicious.

Ultimately, out of fear, the old king forbade citizens to meet, walk together, or eat together. There were spies set everywhere in the cities and on the roads, to watch to see if anyone met contrary to the king's orders. Offenders were taken to the citadel Hyrcania, never to be seen again.

Once Herod had been a handsome young prince, a splendid athlete, and a dashing warrior, a hero worthy of his name. As he grew old he tried to arrest the erosion of the years. His clothes and jewelry remained beautiful.

Although he dyed his hair as black as it had ever been, he could do nothing about the deterioration inside his head.

By the time Jesus of Nazareth was born the king was dying slowly of a vile disease, and he knew it. He was swollen up with pain and stinking with decay. His mind had fallen into worse disarray than his body, That was the year he ordered his sons by Mariamme strangled. He made his eldest son his new heir apparent, but before long he had him killed, too.

A Child Is Born

Leaders among the Pharisees saw in the reign of King Herod a judgment of god which Jews were under an obligation to bear patiently. However, most of those who acquiesced did so only in the hope that their god would soon grant relief by sending a messiah to deliver them.

According to many teachers the kingdom of god was at hand. There is among their scriptures a mystical book predicting when it will come, written by a prophet named Daniel. Daniel prophesied the coming of the messiah, whom he called *the Son of Man*, seventy weeks after Cyrus the King of Persia ordered the Temple in Jerusalem to be rebuilt. This was construed by scholars to mean weeks of years, rather than days. The 490 years ran out just eleven years before the coronation of Herod the Great. By then strange notions were gaining currency. All manner of political events and natural happenings were being analyzed as to how they related to the fulfillment of that prophecy. Respected authorities expressed the opinion that the appearance of the messiah could take place at any time.

Among the Jews a hopeful fervor was developing. The advent of the Son of Man was being anticipated impatiently. Specifically, the birth of a savior was expected. The prophet Isaiah had written, "Unto us a child is born, unto us a son is given; and the government shall be upon his shoulder; and his name shall be called wonderful, counselor, the mighty God, the everlasting Father, the Prince of Peace." These are stirring words to the Jews. It was into a roiling ferment that Jesus of Nazareth was born in the latter years of the reign of Caesar Augustus, in the mountain village of Bethlehem of Judea.

A number of incendiary factors joined to ignite the flame that became Christianity, which is now burning in the arena among the ashes of Rome.

The first was the fact that a general census for tax purposes was under way in Judea at the time he was born. His supposed father, a carpenter named Joseph from the town of Nazareth in Galilee, had to take his pregnant betrothed wife to Bethlehem, the city of the great King David of long ago. It is a small town built of tawny native stone on the ridge of one of the rocky Judean hills, seven miles south of Jerusalem. Joseph happened to be descended in a direct line from King David. He probably went to Bethlehem because he had inherited an interest in some property in the city of his forefathers.

The law requires that the owners of property in Judea must appear and pay the taxes upon it in the jurisdiction in which the property is located. Presumably that is why Joseph had to be numbered with his wife there in Bethlehem.

The reason the location of the birth of the child was important is that one of the Jewish prophets predicted that the messiah would be born in Bethlehem. All agreed he was to be directly descended from King David, so that accident of location was important among the various factors connected with his birth which contributed to what would come to pass later.

If he had been born a few weeks earlier or later, in Nazareth, chances are he would have lived out a normal life as a carpenter there and died in due time, mourned by family and a few friends.

Another incendiary spark was struck by the fates at the time of his birth. As chance would have it, he was born on the occasion of an unusual phenomenon. It was what seemed to be a new bright star.

It is said that the destinies of men are determined more by the stars than by the designs of themselves or others. This was certainly true of Jesus of Nazareth, though in a peculiar way. It was by that star that the course of his life was charted.

Let me first explain that it was apparently the result of a conjoining of Saturn and Jupiter, so that together they almost appeared to be one bright star in the constellation of Pisces. Certainly such a conjunction took place at the right time, and I assume that it was the origin of the story of the star of Bethlehem.

If so, three astrologers who came to Jerusalem from the East were responsible for making an omen of that natural incident. In the new Christian lore they are called the *three wise men*. It is likely that they were Jews from Babylonia. I assume that they were Jews because of the interest they evinced in the birth of a king of the Jews. Who but Jews would come on a spiritual pilgrimage to see a Jewish prince? I infer their Babylonian origin because in the East, astrology is chiefly practiced among Babylonians, and there has been a large Jewish population in that area ever since King Nebuchadnezzar carried off the Jewish people into captivity.

According to Babylonian doctrine about the stars, Pisces represents the West. Jewish tradition makes Pisces both the sign of Israel and the sign of the messiah.

There is yet another sort of symbolism involved. Pisces is at the end of the old passage of the sun and at the beginning of the new one. Therefore astrologers in various countries read into the appearance of the star an omen of the passing of an old era and the beginning of a new age. As those few who are old enough to remember the event may recall, Roman seers explained it as the harbinger of a period of greater glory for Rome under the rule of Caesar Augustus. Their reputations were, as a result, enhanced by what took place during the years that followed.

The two specific stars involved in the conjunction are highly symbolic to all peoples, of course. Jupiter is universally held to be a star of good fortune and a royal star. Saturn has been equated with the god of the Jews from times long past. Furthermore, the Babylonians teach that Saturn is the star of Judea and Syria. For these reasons, the three astrologers took the star to be the sign of the birth of a future Jewish king. The Christian accounts report that the three arrived in Jerusalem asking, "Where is he who is born to be King of the Jews? We have seen his star from afar and have come to worship him."

Their appearance and their question disturbed Herod the Great. The kingdom had been troubled by rumors spread by Pharisees that their god had revealed his decision to bring Roman rule to an end in Judea. A sign from heaven would announce the coming of the new king, they said, aggravating old Herod no end.

On hearing of the arrival in Jerusalem of the three magi and the question they were asking innocently, the king called the chief priests and scribes together and asked them where the great king would be born. They quoted a Jewish prophet named Micah that the ruler of Israel would come out of Bethlehem.

With that information, Herod summoned the three pilgrims to his palace, (where I lived in later years when in Jerusalem). When they appeared before him, he told them they should go to Bethlehem. He directed them to send word back to him when they found the newborn king, in order that he might come and pay homage, too. They responded to this interest on the part of the old king with suspicion. The Christians have cause to call them the three wise men. When they learned that the future king they had come to worship was not a child of Herod's household, they anticipated that bloody old man would do whatever might be necessary to make sure his heirs would be secure on the throne of Judea.

They were on their short journey from Jerusalem southward to Bethlehem when the stars conjoined once again, some two months after the first occurrence. As they traveled, the star appeared before them, over the city of Bethlehem. This was taken to be a sign from their god. It is much spoken of among Christians.

The astrologers found Joseph and Mary and presented gifts of gold, myrrh, and frankincense. These must have been sent by Jews in Babylonia. Probably some sort of collection was taken up there when the meaning of the star was construed as it was. The three men remained for some time worshipping the newborn child. When they departed to return to their own country, they did not go by way of Jerusalem, having correctly divined the basis of the king's interest in the child.

When he heard they had flouted his commands, King Herod was furious. He had not hesitated to kill his favorite wife and children on the basis of suspicion alone in the past, and he did not falter now. He ordered that all of the male infants in Bethlehem and its environs be slaughtered.

By this decision the King helped to compound the future problem. Because a slaughter of the sons of Bethlehem was described in the scriptures of the Jews, both the birth and the massacre were taken later to be a fulfillment of prophecy by those who were so inclined.

Herod's action then was the third circumstance associated with the birth of Jesus that contributed to the legend that later developed. Joseph, having been forewarned in some manner, perhaps by the wise men, fled with Mary and her child down the coast into Egypt, a traditional haven for Jews in times of trouble. There are many villages of Jews in the delta of the Nile. They probably sojourned among their countrymen in one of those hamlets or in the Jewish quarter of the city of Alexandria. It is not surprising that the deliverance of the child came to be viewed by those disposed to do so as an act of the Jewish god. It appeared that Herod had attempted to thwart the will of their god by trying to kill the child, but that their god had intervened to save him.

An ancient prophet called Hosea put into the mouth of their god the words, "I have called my Son out of Egypt." So yet another prophecy seemed to be fulfilled as an indirect result of the action of King Herod.

To those basic elements others were added to heighten the effect. There are stories about the birth of Jesus of Nazareth that are quite fantastic. One given wide circulation among Christians tells of the appearance in the night sky of messengers from their god called angels, which the Pharisees believe in though the Sadducees do not. These angels were supposed to have appeared to shepherds in the fields below Bethlehem to announce the birth of the child. Then they reportedly filled the heavens with hymns of praise to the newborn king. Everyone, except the Christians, assumes that this story was invented later by someone to supplement the legend, along with a number of other items.

It has been suggested that those fortuitous coincidences which undoubtedly did surround Jesus's birth were pondered by Joseph and Mary, and they came to think that they might be able to make a great man of this first-born son, and that they might through him promote the cause of the Jewish people, if he should develop the ability and intelligence to capitalize upon his portentous beginnings.

No one can know their motives, but the effects of their actions were profound. Joseph and Mary talked privately about other angels as well. They claimed that messengers from their god appeared to them both, separately, to foretell the birth of Jesus, and to inform each of them that the unborn child was the messiah.

Each reported that the angel which appeared said to call the baby Yeshua, after Joshua, a general who had led the Jews in their conquest of Palestine long ago. The name is a symbolic one. It means *God saves*. In Greek it becomes *Jesus*.

Joseph said that the angel appeared to him in a dream to tell him that he should not hesitate to marry the woman, even though she was pregnant. The angel assured him, he said, that she was a virgin and that the child was the only begotten son of their god. Mary reported a similar appearance, and added that she was told he would reign over Israel forever.

However much others might smile at this tale of a child born to a virgin, the Christians take it as seriously as Romans take the story of Hercules being born to Alcmene and great Jupiter. It seems clear that Jesus himself believed it. He must have heard it early in his life, as there is an account which I shall give later of his referring to the Jewish god as "my father" while still in his childhood.

There are also some strange tales told among Christians about the birth of another infant in Judea a few months earlier. This child was another who would be accepted as the messiah by some Jews. He would become a famous prophet called John the Baptist. His mother, a previously barren woman named Elizabeth, happened to be a cousin to Mary. His father was an elderly priest of the Temple in Jerusalem called Zacharias.

This Zacharias said that an angel appeared to him in the Temple, while he was performing his priestly offices, to tell him that his wife would conceive and bear a son who would grow up to be a great man of their god.

Those who are not Pharisees and do not believe in angels of a Jewish god, assume that these visions of Zacharias, Joseph, and Mary were either hallucinations or fabrications. I presume that word of any experience as remarkable as that claimed by Zacharias would have been communicated to members of his family by one means or another, even to those in Galilee, three days away.

The story he told might have suggested similar ones to Mary and Joseph. I have already explained that the alleged appearance of the angel to Joseph was supposed to have been in a dream. As we all have noticed, in our own experiences, though some dreams are portentous messages from some supernatural being or another, some are not. There are dreams which just flow from occurrences or situations in our lives, from whatever is on our minds or on our shoulders. It would not be surprising if the tale told by Zacharias had triggered just such a dream during the troubled sleep of Joseph, as was pointed out to me when I first heard the story, while I was still in Palestine. After all, having your beloved

• 31 •

become pregnant does not tend to promote peaceful sleep. Certainly the reasons are obvious why Mary might have produced such a story. As to the paternity of her child, I shall comment later upon the view of the Jewish religious establishment on that question.

It is known that Mary spent some time in the home of Zacharias and Elizabeth in the Judean hills when both women were pregnant. They must have talked about their unborn children then. Probably they accepted each others' stories at face value. There is an account of their visit which includes a reference to Elizabeth's having accepted the child to be born to Mary as the messiah, in accordance with Mary's and Joseph's reports of their visions. It may also be assumed that both John the Baptist and Jesus of Nazareth grew up with these stories about themselves and each other.

The actions of Mary and Joseph also added another element to the forces that would send Jesus down the road that would take him to his grave. After about three years in Egypt they heard word of the death of King Herod. They returned then, but not to Judea, which had been bequeathed by the dying king to his son Archelaus. They were as afraid of him as they had been of Herod. So was everyone else.

Instead Mary and Joseph took the child into Galilee, which Herod had left to a son of milder temper, Herod Antipas. The additional element to which I referred was their decision to return to the town of Nazareth. By that action they seemed to fulfill in the child a prediction that the messiah would be a Nazarene. It is not uncommon for parents to contribute to the destruction of their children. Fortunately, the pattern is seldom so imperial.

The Boy Becomes A Carpenter

Jesus grew up in Nazareth, a town about an hour's walk away from Sepphoris, which was then the largest city in Galilee, as well as the seat of the government of the tetrarch, Herod Antipas. As a suburb of a busy Jewish capital city, Nazareth was caught up in a greater world than most of the small towns in the countryside of Southern Galilee.

Nazareth is located in an amphitheater of hills just to the north of the Valley of Esdraelon. The Via Maris passes through that valley on the way from Africa to Syria, Parthia, and Babylon. Caravans of camels can be seen from the hills around Nazareth on most days, carrying the wealth of nations over the most famous road of the East.

In Jewish towns like Nazareth, the council of elders of the synagogue also rules the town. The boy Jesus grew up under a religious government that applied the principles of Judaism to every aspect of life. Such regimes pattern themselves after the type of theocracy that ruled the nation of Israel in times past, and which Jews hope for once again with the coming of the messiah.

The elders of Nazareth arranged for the education of every Jewish boy in the town. From their cradles Jews are taught by their elders to believe in their god as the creator of the earth and the father of mankind. In their early years at home, they learn ancient prayers from their fathers, beginning with the *shema*, a prayer which is recited morning and evening by every Jew, "Hear, O Israel, the Lord our God, the Lord is one." At the age of six or seven, boys are sent to village schools. I have often seen them sitting in the shade of an old tree, attending to their masters as the world passed by.

After he took to the highways as a roving prophet, Jesus showed an unusual knowledge of the Jewish law. From that I conclude that he also went to a Pharisaic school where his education in religious subjects would have been more thorough. I suppose Joseph would have pressed to get him into such a school, to prepare him to fulfill the destiny predicted for him by the three astrologers. There he would have learned Hebrew, which was the national tongue of the Jews before the Babylonian captivity. It is still taught because the reading of the ancient scriptures is a sacred duty among Jews. In their education the holy scrolls are the only ones used. They must memorize psalms of King David and proverbs of King Solomon, as well as many passages from the various prophets. They are required to know by heart the long history of their people, all the way back into the legendary past.

In school the boys sit attentively and repeat the lessons of their masters until they have them committed to memory. The masters are specialists in the law. The education they provide is principally instruction in legal matters, in accordance with the precepts of the Pharisees. This indoctrination of the leaders of each new generation with their own articles of faith is one of the reasons for the increasing ascendancy of the doctrines of the Pharisees over those of the Sadducees. So Jesus undoubtedly was brought up to believe in a life after death.

The Pharisees taught him that a Jew should take pleasure in complying with the law, because every time he did it he would be serving his god. The importance they assign to learning the law is set forth in a letter by the apostle of Jesus named Paul, a Pharisee himself. He said, "Study to show thyself approved unto God, a workman who does not need to be ashamed, rightly dividing the word of truth." The legal education Jesus would have received in such a school was as thorough as the training given lawyers in most countries. As I have earlier mentioned, the technicalities of the Jewish code are many.

In today's world everyone knows that the Jews will not work on the seventh day of the week. This seems a simple rule to Romans. It is welcomed by the lower classes who have accepted it as a good custom. The contrary view of the patricians, who are offended by the indolence and sloth it represents, was expressed by Seneca when he said of the Jews, "This abominable nation has succeeded in spreading its customs throughout all lands; the conquered have given their laws to the conquerors."

However, a boy like Jesus would have learned that the observance of the sabbath day is not the simple matter of taking the day off from one's regular employment that Romans take it to be. Like almost every part of the Jewish law as interpreted by the Pharisees, this rule is detailed and precise.

Thirty-nine primary works of man are enumerated and are prohibited on the sabbath. They include such activities as sowing, reaping, plowing, grinding, kneading, washing, building, the tying of knots, and the lighting of fires. There are, in addition, a myriad of minor works that are forbidden as well.

Each of the thirty-nine chief works is defined and governed in the law. The provisions relating to any of them would serve to demonstrate the complexities of the rules. For the sake of brevity, it will be best to use a simple example, like the tying of knots.

Pharisees teach their students that only certain knots make a man guilty of breaking the sabbath. Those of sailors and camel drivers are forbidden, but no sin is committed in the tying of a knot which can be undone with one hand. A woman may tie the strings of her cap, her girdle, or her shoes, or the strings that close up skins of wine or oil. Thus, if a Jew wishes to secure two things together on the sabbath, he can have his wife tie them to each other with her girdle without impiety, while he would be breaking the law if he did it himself with a cord.

In such a school Jesus would have had these rules etched into his mind by endless repetitions, by an exacting master. He would have been called upon to memorize the legal points that are important to the Pharisees who try to make every act a part of a holy ritual. He would have learned that no food may be prepared on the sabbath. That meant having to know the rules as to which steps that bring food to the table are to be considered preparation and which are not. What should be a simple concept, the distinction between cooking food and merely warming it, is defined at length and becomes a very fine and tortuous line.

In such a school he would have learned hundreds of provisions of law about which types of vessels, utensils, tools, and furniture can be defiled and which cannot. He would have had to be able to define and categorize every type of object and the rules pertaining to it. He would have learned that a flat plate with a rim could be defiled, a flat plate without a rim could not; a round horn could be, a straight horn could not. A wooden key with iron teeth was susceptible but an iron key with wooden teeth was not, or perhaps it was the other way around. A stove would be defiled if wood from a grove sacred to a Roman god burned in it. An old stove could be purified while a new stove must be broken.

In such a school he would have been taught the various classifications of water: pond water, collected water, running water, and spring water, which in turn were divided into categories, depending upon whether the spring was a running spring or not, and how much it produced. He would have been informed as to the degree to which any variety of water may be diluted, if at all, by any other specific type of water, for any particular use.

I fear that my trying to indicate the complexity of the Jewish law by giving instances of its singularities must be futile. The examples must be so few; and there is an implication in an attempt at explanation that it is possible to impart an understanding of the subject in a brief space. In fact, it would take many volumes to set forth all the law that would have been taught to Jesus in such a school. He must have learned all these things, but at the same time he also would have been told that an empty formal compliance with the law was not sufficient, according to the prophets.

The curriculum contained no secular matter. Thus young Jews are denied the civilizing influences of classical literature, philosophy, and various other intellectual activities. Sometimes they learn the elements of arithmetic, depending on the skills of the teacher; however, their education in the orderly science of mathematics does not go beyond that. The beautiful logic of Pythagoras and Euclid is not employed to discipline their thinking.

Unlike the Greeks and Romans, the Jews do not organize athletic activities for growing boys. Jesus and his young friends played in the narrow streets, as children everywhere do, but their games did not make up a part of their formal education for the development of character, as is the case with us.

While all this intensive education was going forward, later events suggest that Joseph and Mary were spinning for him their stories of the star and the angels, filling his young mind with visions of the most mystical nature.

As a boy he learned the trade of carpentry. Jewish law makes it the obligation of a boy's father to teach him a livelihood. He started in the shop of Joseph, cleaning up the sweet smelling wood chips and shavings, running errands, and doing other menial jobs. In the course of doing his chores, and dreaming his dreams, he picked up the skills of his trade, as boys have been learning from their fathers from time immemorial throughout the earth.

Fulfilling another legal obligation, the carpenter took the boy to synagogue with him in the forenoon of every sabbath. The Jewish service consists of prayers, a reading of the *Torah*, and a reading from the prophets, in Hebrew. After each scripture reading they would have heard a translation into Aramaic and a discourse upon it. With Joseph beside him, the lad must have listened intently to the promises about the messiah and the golden age he would bring to his people as their lord and king, turning in his mind the stories about his own birth in Bethlehem, as Joseph must have been doing, too. At the close of the service there is a blessing by a priest. The prayers, preaching, and scripture reading are undertaken by members of the congregation appointed each week by the officials of the synagogue. When Jesus returned later as a wandering preacher to the place where he had worshipped as boy, he served in that role.

Jews also meet on the mornings of the second and fifth days of the week, when only the *Torah* is read. At other seasons of the year there are many other special meetings. Jewish services involve worship, of course, but the emphasis is on explaining the law.

Yet the instruction they receive in school and synagogue should not be considered the extent of the religious education of Jews in a place like Nazareth. All Jews are admonished that it is a reproach to them if they ever sit down to eat without discoursing upon the law with anyone who may be present. And they pray daily at appointed times.

They eat, sleep, and breathe their religion and the law. They live for it or die for it as the occasion demands. Their religious attitudes are hard for us to understand. A Roman will die willingly for a cause, or for Rome, or for honor, or just to show he is not afraid to, but would any Roman die for a god? Hardly. Being a pragmatic people, Romans are disposed to be broad-minded about gods.

For relaxation, a family from Nazareth might walk into the city of Sepphoris. Probably Joseph took his family there fairly often. I have heard that Mary was born there and that her family lived there in those days.

In the markets of the great city they could see exotic foreigners selling the products of far-away lands. A longer walk down into the nearby town of Nain in the Valley of Esdraelon would take them among the caravanseries of world trade, to observe the merchants and camel drivers of many nations passing through on the Via Maris.

As a boy Jesus would have learned that these travellers were devotees of mystery faiths of the East that involve resurrected saviors. Naturally, the Egyptians made the valley ring with the praises of Osiris, the Lord of Lords, whose return to life they celebrate so joyously. Just as they do now, the more pious among the Greeks rejoiced over Adonis rising from the grave, during their annual festival.

The Syrians travelling between Egypt and Palmyra would have joined the merchants from Babylon in raising their voices in praise of Tammuz, the husband of Ishtar, who died at her hands and rose again after three days and ascended into heaven. They greet mankind with the cry "The Lord is risen" in late spring when they celebrate his resurrection. It puts faithful Jews in mind of Baal, the god of the ancient Canaanites they had dispossessed of their lands, who was also supposed to have died and risen again.

The worship of Tammuz was singled out as an abomination in the eyes of the Jewish god by an ancient prophet of theirs named Ezekiel during the time of the Babylonian captivity of the Jews. The spread of the popularity of Tammuz from Babylon to the adjacent lands of Syria and Phoenicia troubles them now as much as a revival of the rites of Baal would do.

Such faiths were discussed with great disapproval by the Jews in their synagogues and homes. It is important to remember in connection with the story of Jesus of Nazareth that any movement among the Jews that has to do with a resurrected savior will cause the religious authorities to suspect that it was derived from foreign religions that they abhor.

Because it probably affected the development of some of Jesus's attitudes, I should add a word here about the economic state of Galilee, and Palestine in general, during his childhood. Although the benefits of Roman rule have never been admitted by most Jews, they certainly were conscious of enjoying an orderly economy and stable government under the principate of Caesar Augustus. The best roads the East had ever known were being laid down, making overland commerce prosper. The seas had been made safe from pirates, and maritime trade was flourishing. Roman soldiers maintained order and business prospered. There was peace.

Moreover, within an otherwise evenhanded system, Jews of Nazareth like Joseph and his son were aware that their people were being treated differently from other nations subject to Roman rule. This first came to pass as a result of decrees of Julius Caesar, who granted them many concessions related to their faith. No people mourned the death of Caesar more sincerely or vocally.

These concessions were renewed as a result of the close friendship Herod the Great cultivated with Caesar Augustus and Marcus Agrippa. After voluntarily joining Agrippa with a large force in a hard campaign on the north shores of the Euxine, Herod prevailed upon him to confirm the laws of the Jews. Their code forbade the Jews to appear in court on the seventh day of the week. Like Caesar before him, Agrippa excused them from such appearances. The problem of the sabbath, when joined to the laws relating to diet, which are as full of niceties as all of their other laws, made it impossible for Jews to serve in the Roman armies. Therefore, young Jews like Jesus were exempted from conscription, first by Caesar and later by Agrippa.

These were singular concessions which continue in effect to this day, to the indignation of most other peoples. Jews in Nazareth were full of the knowledge that both Julius Caesar and Caesar Augustus, the two greatest men of the age, acknowledged the special position of the Jews among the peoples of the world.

During this peaceful interlude in a troubled history,

the fact that Jews were far better off than in the past did not diminish the hope for an early advent of a messiah, a hope that burned as brightly as the kitchen fire in every Jewish home.

As unpopular as King Herod had been, his death had come as a blow to the people of Nazareth just as it did to Jews everywhere else, because all semblance of a national existence expired with him. The old king's last will divided his kingdom into three parts among three of his sons. Archelaus, who enjoyed a fierce reputation like that of his father, was left Judea, Samaria, and Idumea. These lands were confirmed to him by a decree of Caesar Augustus, with the title of *ethnarch*, which is a little less than *king*.

This decision occasioned a revolt in Jerusalem despite the efforts of a Pharisee named Hillel, the President of the Sanhedrin, to prevent it. He counseled the Jews to accept the authority of government as the will of god. The zealots would not listen to him. The uprising was so serious that it required the intervention of Varus, who was then Governor of Syria, to suppress it. Ultimately he crucified over two thousand Jews on a small forest of crosses around the city walls.

Nazareth passed under the rule of Herod Antipas, who received all of Galilee and Perea. Herod Philip, the third brother, got the rest of the lands beyond the Jordan. Herod Antipas and Herod Philip were given the designation *tetrarch*, which is a little less than *ethnarch*. The title of *King of the Jews* died with Herod the Great and the dismemberment of his kingdom. It only reappeared once, like a theatrical ghost flittering across the stage, during the brief reign of King Herod Agrippa twenty years ago.

One other effect of the division of the kingdom by the will of King Herod was that the jurisdiction of the Great

Sanhedrin in Jerusalem was limited to the dominions of Archelaus. After that time the lands ruled by Herod Antipas and Herod Philip were not subject to that court, a fact which must be remembered to understand certain aspects of the story of Jesus Christ.

All semblance of Jewish independence was dispelled when Archelaus was deposed by Caesar Augustus, in response to protests against the king's tyranny that were raised by the leading men of Judea. His realm was then made a Roman province. It was designated as a land requiring active defense, because of its proximity to Parthia, and was therefore to be governed by a representative of Caesar, as commander-in-chief of the army, rather than by a civil governor appointed by the Senate. It was given over to the rule of Coponius, the first of a long line.

Much as they may have preferred it to the despotism of Archelaus, it was difficult for the Jews to accept the rule of a Roman prefect, except on a temporary basis. A restlessness began to develop which broke out into disorder in my own time there. It has continued to intensify with the passing years as the permanence of direct Roman rule has become more apparent.

Then as now, the Jews, including those who worshipped with Joseph and Jesus in the synagogue in Nazareth, felt oppressed because they were subjects of a people who do not worship their god. They were told that it was because they were sinful that they were unhappy. Upon their repentance and conformity to their god's will depended the freedom of his chosen people and their holy land from the rule of ungodly men like me.

In Galilee Herod Antipas ruled from the time Joseph and Mary brought their infant son to Nazareth. He inherited more of his father's cunning and less of the old king's ferocity than Archelaus did. He took care not to invite hostility to himself as his brother had done. Yet the unrest in Galilee paralleled that in Judea. Like his father, Herod Antipas was seen as an agent of the Roman Empire, and an obstacle to Jewish autonomy.

The tetrarch in all his considerable splendor was seen from time to time by Jesus, growing up on the outskirts of Sepphoris. From the tone of his comments after he became a public figure, it is clear that the carpenter was not brought up to have much respect for Herod.

When Jesus was about twelve years old there was a great uprising in Galilee against the domination of Rome and the rule of Herod Antipas. It was occasioned by a general census for tax purposes. The revolt was led by a zealot from the city of Gamala called Judas of Galilee. This would-be messiah was the son of the rebel Hezekiah whom Herod the Great had beheaded almost half a century earlier. It was this extra-legal execution that had brought Herod into his historic conflict with the Great Sanhedrin, it will be remembered from the introductory chapter.

Raising the war cry, "No ruler but God," Judas called on the Jews of Galilee to dedicate themselves to their god and his kingdom, and to make military action the evidence of their consecration. He was accepted by many as a new Judas Maccabee. Men from Nazareth joined him, religious friends of Joseph and his family, and members of their own synagogue, whom they never saw again. Judas seized control of the city of Sepphoris, which welcomed him. He was able to equip his followers with weapons and military stores from the arsenal in the palace of Herod there. Under his direction the rebels improved the defenses of the city, expecting that their god would intervene to save them.

The tetrarch called for the aid of Rome. After the inevitably successful Roman siege of the city and the slaughter of the rebel garrison, Sepphoris was burned in retribution for the support the people there gave to Judas. The inhabitants were sold off into slavery as punishment. This was a powerful example to set, because, while Jews are permitted to own slaves, they are not much inclined to it, and they have an especial aversion to being enslaved themselves. It is a feeling derived from their high opinion of themselves as the chosen people of their god.

The people of Nazareth and other nearby towns still mourn for their lost friends and former neighbors, resenting what befell them. But they learned an unforgettable lesson in the invincibility of Roman arms. The children who grew up with Jesus in Nazareth still hope for divine deliverance from Roman rule, I have no doubt, but they are not inclined to the view that the proper way of securing the kingdom of god is to invite such another disaster.

As a boy in a neighboring town, Jesus witnessed the disturbing events of the time. From the carpenter shop the lad saw the brass and iron-bound legions of Rome passing in the narrow street on their way to destroy the great city he knew so well. Those soldiers were in and around Nazareth all during the siege. They were stern and implacable veterans, the kind of men who would stamp a lasting impression on a boy's mind.

Jesus also beheld in the street distraught friends and relatives, old and young, as they were led weeping through Nazareth into slavery from the ruins of Sepphoris. Not even the star of Bethlehem could have been more in the minds of the family of Joseph than the fate of their neighbors.

Ten years after the destruction of his capital city, Herod Antipas undertook to restore it on a scale more grand and beautiful than before. Although it is now called the ornament of all Galilee, its new splendor serves as a monumental reminder of past tragedy to the Jews in the area.

The reconstruction commenced after Jesus had grown to manhood, during the years when he was still working at his trade. If he did not work in Sepphoris, he surely observed the progress of construction, and was reminded throughout his young manhood how Galileans had accepted the claim of Judas of Galilee that he was the long awaited messiah and had paid an awful price for doing it.

Probably the fate of the city of Sepphoris shaped the attitudes of Jesus of Nazareth toward Rome. He indicated that he understood the futility of rebellion in all that he said toward the close of his life.

It was at the time that the rebuilding of Sepphoris commenced that Caesar Augustus died. The world mourned the passing of the god who had ruled it for half a century, who had brought order and prosperity and peace. Like every nation the Jews approved his words to the friends gathered around his death bed at Nola, "Since I have played my part well, clap your hands, and with applause dismiss me from the stage."

The people of Nazareth did not want to be ruled by a Roman Emperor, of course, but they had come to accept status quo because they had no choice, and they were willing to applaud the memory of Augustus in appreciation for the privileges he and his great-uncle had granted them. Young men like Jesus and old men like Joseph were concerned about the future. They feared that the new government of Tiberius, the stern warrior, might not be so favorably disposed towards them, and they were right.

With one exception, there appears to have been nothing preserved in the way of anecdotes about the youth or childhood of Jesus. The agents of the Great

Sanhedrin who later investigated his background reported that his early years were spent in obscurity as a witness to the disturbing events which transpired around him.

The one story which is current among Christians about a specific episode in his childhood relates that, when he was twelve years of age, on the threshold of manhood according to Jewish custom, Joseph and Mary took him to Jerusalem for Passover. This is a festival marked by the custom of eating unleavened bread and sacrificial lambs to celebrate the deliverance of the Jews from slavery in Egypt in the time of Moses. It commemorates the miraculous works allegedly done by their god on their behalf to liberate them from foreign bondage. It also looks forward to the future wonders that will accompany their ultimate salvation upon the coming of the messiah. It brings hundreds of thousands of Jewish pilgrims from all over the East to Jerusalem, including a considerable percentage of the population of Judea and Galilee.

Jews are expressly commanded to rejoice at their festivals, yet, like all other Jewish feasts, Passover would seem to Romans to be a very serious affair. It is given over to earnest prayers and sober worship. And what feasting they do is not done for the pure pleasure of it; it is just another element of their rituals.

They have no merry gods like Bacchus, and their one god is terribly serious at every season of the year. They have no festivals in which they see him in a joyful mood, no revelries when an ordinary man can abandon himself to the satisfaction of his appetites with whatever man or woman who takes his fancy. Many a Roman in Judea has felt that, if those bearded puritans could loosen up and celebrate one good Saturnalia, it would diminish the problem they present to themselves and to the world.

Joseph and Mary were part of a large company of people when they left Jerusalem on the road home to Galilee after the close of the feast. Their boy had not come with the party, as they had every reason to expect him to do, but they were not aware of it because there was such a throng of travelers with them. It was not until the end of the first day's journey, when they sought him everywhere among their kinsfolk and acquaintances, that they became alarmed.

They returned to the city in the morning. After three days they found him in the courts of the Temple, sitting among the learned men there, listening to them, asking questions, and answering them. According to the story, all who heard him were impressed with his wisdom and his understanding.

His mother Mary reproached him for causing them so much anxiety. Very seriously he replied to her, "Why have you sought me? Don't you know I must be about my father's business?"

This story must have given her an indication of the direction in which his mind had been turned even at that age. The consequences of her own and Joseph's stories about his birth were becoming apparent. It would be interesting to know what was in her mind when she heard his answer

In that year a powerful leader among the Sadducees named Annas officiated as High Priest. Either he or members of his family have filled that office, with only an occasional interlude, throughout the half century and more since. Annas played an important role in the trial and execution of Jesus over twenty years later. Some have wondered whether Annas was among those who talked with him in the temple that day, and whether the old High Priest remembered that serious young boy when Jesus was conducted into his chambers for interrogation the night before he died on the cross.

A Wayside Prophet

Most of his life Jesus followed his trade in the town of Nazareth, as far as I know. Nowadays, Christians say that this, too, corresponds with the prophecies of Jewish scriptures, which state that the messiah would live many years unrecognized and in humble circumstances. Most Jews suggest that that can be said of so many men it can hardly be claimed as a criterion for the identification of Jesus as the messiah.

One day he was a carpenter, the next day he was a prophet. He first came to the attention of the Jewish religious hierarchy and the civil authorities during the fifteenth year of the reign of Tiberius, when he joined his cousin John the Baptist, who had become an itinerant preacher in Perea, beyond the Jordan River.

John was a remarkable figure. Wearing a camel's hair cloak and a leather belt he appeared out of the desert, where he had subsisted on a diet of wild honey and grasshoppers. These insects are eaten by the mean and lowly in the East, generally boiled, with the legs and heads pulled off.

Denouncing evil in high places, John called upon the Jews to be baptised in the Jordan River, as a sign of repentance for their sins. He was a striking figure of a man, with long hair and beard like the ancient prophets of Israel. A great number of Jews came to consider John to be a prophet of their god; and he is still widely so accepted. Although he denied it himself, there were those who arrived at the conclusion that John himself was the messiah. Consequently the agents of Herod Antipas and the Great Sanhedrin in Jerusalem undertook to keep close track of him. Even though John did not carry on his activities in Judea, I was kept informed about him in Caesarea, because any potential messianic movement could affect Jews in one jurisdiction as well as the other.

John caused a disturbance in the public mind when he announced that the Roman Empire and the rights of the Herodian lines of royalty would all be set aside in a new kingdom soon to be established by the Jewish god. He declared himself to be the herald of the new king, saying, "I am the voice of one crying in the wilderness, prepare ye the way of the Lord."

Although John was not a political zealot like Judas of Galilee, his proclamations stirred up unrest. Herod Antipas began to fear that his movement might develop revolutionary tendencies. For this reason John was locked up in the fortress of Machaerus, as well as for his denunciation of the illegal marriage of Herod to his niece Herodias, who was also his brother's wife. John was beheaded in time, chiefly for having enraged Herodias.

At first it seemed that the carpenter was just another of John's many disciples, only to be distinguished from the others by the fact that he happened to be John's cousin. However, when Jesus of Nazareth presented himself for baptism, John protested and said, "It is I who should be baptised by you."

One of the miraculous stories about Jesus is told in connection with his baptism. It is to the effect that the spirit of the Jewish god appeared as a dove and said, "This is my son, in whom I am well pleased."

Like the legend of the angels appearing at the scene of his birth, this tale is believed by Christians but by no one else. Obviously if these stories had been widely accepted among Jews and Romans, his story would have been a different one with a different ending.

Be that as it may, John made it clear that Jesus was the lord whose appearance he proclaimed. John's mother had accepted Jesus as the messiah when he was yet unborn. Presumably John was brought up to that belief, as Jesus was himself.

John said of his cousin, "Behold the Lamb of God who takes away the sins of the world." In saying this, he was referring to one of the psalms of King David which says, "The Lord hath laid upon Him the iniquity of us all ... He is brought as a lamb to the slaughter."

The remark about Jesus being the Lamb of God foretold the course of his life, though we did not know it at the time. Jewish scriptures say that forgiveness of sin normally requires a blood sacrifice. Jesus' acceptance of the role of the ultimate sacrificial lamb, ascribed to him by John, explains much of what he later did.

Since John the Baptist did not consider him to be just another disciple, the religious authorities did not either. Devout Jews took an interest in Jesus of Nazareth when John declared him to be the one whose appearance he had come to foretell.

Like John, who preached his message in Perea, Jesus chose to commence his ministry within the domain of Herod Antipas. The tetrarch could be expected to be more tolerant of self-styled prophets than the Great Sanhedrin in Jerusalem would be.

Jesus returned to Galilee and took up residence in the city of Capernaum, which is pleasantly situated on the north shore of the Lake of Tiberias, or the Sea of Galilee, as the Jews continue to call it. He assembled a band of disciples, unlettered fishermen mostly, and began to wander about the Galilean countryside preaching. He appeared in the smaller towns. He spoke in the fields and on the hills. He avoided Tiberias, the new capital of Galilee, because it had been built in part over an old cemetery and was therefore an unclean place.

Tiberias has a mixed population because righteous Jews will not live on such ground. Because during those early months Jesus was appealing only to Jews, he was limiting his appearances to places where the population was Jewish. That also explains why he stayed away from Sepphoris. After its reconstruction it, too, was a place with a motley assortment of inhabitants. His decision to try to reach the Jews first must have been the cause for his avoiding the Greek cities of the Decapolis region as well.

In every large crowd that assembled in Galilee or Perea the spies and informers of Herod Antipas circulated. They reported that the carpenter was making a great impression everywhere. The Jews had been exposed to other wandering prophets in recent years, but no one quite like him. He attracted listeners with an ethereal self-assurance. Then he moved them with a peculiar oratorical talent. In his sermons he often spoke mysteriously, complying it seemed with the phrase from Jewish scripture, "I will speak in parables, I will utter dark sayings of old."

Like most religious leaders among the Jews, he concerned himself with the coming of the kingdom of heaven. He made the thought of his god as the loving father of mankind the foundation of his teachings.

The kingdom of heaven, he taught, involves the rule of the Jewish god in the hearts of men. It is to be sought by discerning the will of that god, and by demonstrating a faithful obedience in everything we do. Much of what he said was in accordance with the teachings of the Pharisees, especially when he set forth what he considered to be the proper ways for a man to conform his actions to the will of their god.

For example, Jesus said, "Do unto others what you would have them do unto you." A few years before, the most respected leader among the Pharisees, Hillel, had expressed the same gentle, impractical sentiment in almost the same words. Hillel said, "What is hateful to you do not do unto another; this is the whole law, the rest is commentary."

Jesus went further. He commanded his followers to love their enemies, to return good for evil, to bless those who curse them, and to pray for those who persecute them. He said, "Whosoever shall strike you upon the right cheek, turn to him the other also. Whosoever shall force you to go a mile with him, go with him two."

The fact that a Roman soldier could require anyone to carry his gear for one mile had always caused resentment among the Jews. To order them to abase themselves by voluntarily going another mile was to call for total humility and submission. By this type of injunction he indicated that he was no threat to the authority of Rome or Herod Antipas.

In trying to evaluate whether I needed to be concerned about this charismatic man, I was reassured by other phrases that were attributed to him, such as "Blessed are the meek, for they shall inherit the earth," and, "Blessed are the peacemakers, for they shall be called the children of God." It appeared that it was probably in Rome's best interests to promote both the man and his message among the Jews, though it would be desirable to prevent the spread of any such concepts among Romans.

These basic premises ruffled no feathers, yet in his early ministry he aroused the hostility of the scribes and Pharisees. The carpenter became a challenge to the established religious institutions when he began to assume the rule of an authoritative teacher among the Jews. The scriptures are explained by scribes and rabbis with hard-earned credentials. It was an offense to the Pharisees that he put himself on a level above the officially qualified teachers of the law.

He advocated a strict sort of religion, as absolute as that of the Pharisees. He set almost impossible standards of righteousness. He held that it is not sufficient to avoid doing evil. For example, he said that a man who lusts after any woman who is not his wife has committed adultery in his heart. The Pharisees felt that men could lead virtuous lives. This man made sinners of everyone, Jews and gentiles alike.

Another disturbing note was sounded when he espoused the Essene principle that rich men should give up their possessions to achieve righteousness. "It is easier for a camel to go through the eye of a needle," he said, "than for a rich man to enter into the kingdom of God." This radical doctrine was looked upon as subversive of society's values, naturally.

What attracted greater notice than the message he preached were the things that he did. Word went out through Galilee, Judea, Perea, and Syria that he was a performer of mighty works. The first story to circulate involved his turning water into wine at a wedding at Cana. Soon I began to pick up a trickle of accounts about him curing leprosy, palsy, dropsy, epilepsy, blindness, deafness, and sundry other complaints.

Jews came from all around bringing their sick to be

cured. The carpenter began to attract attention as a very holy man. Among the Jews the power to heal has always been considered a mark of godly authority in a man. In that opinion they are like most other nations. The reputation of such a god as Aesculapius rests upon the heaps of crutches at his shrine at Epidaurus, discarded by lame people when they walked away cured.

Faith healing is as old as the human race itself. When skeptics suggested that Jesus of Nazareth was not curing real illnesses, but only imagined ones, they were repeating the reservations expressed over the ages about the cures effected by the priests of Aesculapius, Isis, and many another god. Yet in his case there seemed to be more to it than that. It was beyond all normal experiences, according to reports I received.

What made it all the more wonderful to the simple people of the Galilean countryside, he accomplished his cures without requiring his patients to swallow mouse heads, pickled frogs, or any of the other marvelous remedies Eastern physicians prescribe for their unhappy victims. He sounded like the kind of doctor most of us would prefer.

Later I heard other miraculous stories about him that were put forth by his circle of followers. There were ones about how he walked on the water of the Lake of Tiberias, and how he commanded a tempest to cease and it did. His disciples claimed to have witnessed these events themselves.

Were these reports simply stories made up and added to the tales about the angels at his birth, to attract followers to the faith after the man died on the cross? Or did he actually possess the power to work wonders? I shall address that question in the final chapter.

Whatever the truth of the matter may have been, these incredible stories have been causing some heads to shake and others to nod ever since those days when I first heard them in Caesarea.

There is another account of a miracle that was given currency early on, which may actually be two separate stories about an event that took place twice. It has to do with his feeding a multitude that came to hear him preach on the shores of the Lake of Tiberias, with a few loaves and fishes brought by one boy. Doubters suggest that many of the crowd had brought bread and fishes, but had kept them concealed for fear of being expected to share them with those who had no food. They surmise that, when Jesus ordered that the boy's lunch be divided up, others who had food were shamed into adding theirs to the common store. If so, skeptics in my own circle submitted, the miracle was no less remarkable, involving as it did getting those tight-fisted Galileans to share up what they had brought.

Events took a serious turn when the multitude that had been fed responded by proposing to crown him king. Having long awaited a messiah, who was to authenticate himself as their god's representative by working wonders, they thought he had identified himself to them that day.

Many of his listeners had hoped he was a leader who might succeed where Judas of Galilee had failed, and overthrow the tetrarch. When by refusing the crown he made it clear he was not that kind of revolutionary, they turned away from him in disappointment, and Herod relaxed as did I.

More stir was caused by two reports that he had raised the dead to life. One concerned the daughter of a man named Jairus and the other the son of a widow of the city of Nain near Nazareth. These stories were widely repeated. Many common people became convinced that a great prophet had risen among them. Resurrections of the dead were expected to accompany the advent of the messiah.

As to these resurrections, multitudes believed in them, although there were some who were inclined to suspect the risen persons had fainted or had fallen into a coma of some sort. There were also skeptics who suspected both cases were elaborate hoaxes calculated to make the carpenter a great name. Even without the resurrections, the works of Jesus, as they were reported to me in Caesarea, were more impressive than the works of the most noted rabbis or other thaumaturgists of the East.

Before long Jesus of Nazareth was calling himself "The Son of Man," a title used by the prophet Daniel for the coming messiah. Some Jews by then were saying that he was the reincarnation of a great prophet named Elijah.

The Great Sanhedrin in Jerusalem could not ignore these reports of marvellous works by a man making tremendous claims for himself. If his miracles were genuine they might be evidence of divine authority granted to him. On the other hand they might also be the manifestations of some other power. If that were the case, there were steps to be taken.

Always in the minds of the Jews are their laws relating to heresy. Though it is hard to imagine in this modern world, heresy is still a crime among them, punishable by death. The stories about Jesus of Nazareth gripped the attention of the religious authorities. There is a provision in the Jewish law that a false prophet is a preacher of apostasy who seeks to lead Israel astray through magic and deception of the senses, as well as genuine miracles. The false prophet is inspired by the spirit of evil. The wonders he works are done by sorcery, which is in itself a capital crime in Jewish law. His purpose is to beguile the chosen people into incurring the wrath of their god.

The law requires that he who corrupts the people must die, so the corruption will not spread. There is also a general provision that a wicked man must die in order that their god's anger will be lifted from the people.

According to Jewish law every case of apostasy must be corroborated by at least two witnesses. If found guilty, a false prophet must be sentenced by the Great Sanhedrin and put to death by stoning, in the city of Jerusalem.

Pursuant to this law, agents were sent to Capernaum in the early days of the carpenter's career as a wayside prophet to investigate his miracles. The men chosen to make the inquiry were Pharisees and scribes. I soon heard that these theologians made a finding that the miracles and exorcisms performed by Jesus were genuine. The question that remained for them to settle was this: By whose authority were they done? Was the man the long-awaited messiah who would deliver them, or the long-feared deceiver who would lead them to destruction?

It must be remembered how strongly the Pharisees believe in the absolute authority of the law. Only by its strict observance can Israel avoid destruction and achieve its destiny.

To emphasize this point, it will help to quote from the law of Moses, where he gives as the word of their god this warning: "If you break my commandments . . . I will set my face against you. You shall be slain before your enemies: they that hate you shall reign over you. I will scatter you among the heathen . . . and your land shall be desolate and your cities laid waste."

The scribes and Pharisees who came from Jerusalem were disturbed to see that the carpenter was willing to eat and drink in the homes of publicans and sinners. What must be recalled in this connection is their own unwillingness to eat with anyone who is not one of themselves, out of fear that any other host might not have the same knowledge of the law and reverence for it. They thought Jesus was not showing the concern he should to avoid being defiled. They were also attentive to the fact that he did not give evidence of piety by following certain of their customs, including periodic fasting. Jesus tended to resemble Socrates. He apparently felt that it is necessary to be good company to win some men's souls.

The agents of the Sanhedrin were much more seriously disturbed when they saw that some of the disciples of Jesus ate with unwashed hands. They asked him, "Why don't your disciples live according to the traditions of the elders? Instead they eat with their hands defiled."

This was a serious violation of the oral law. The answer Jesus gave raised even more serious questions. He said, "Hear me and understand. There is nothing outside a man which, by going into him, can defile him. What goes into a man cannot defile him, since it enters not his heart but his stomach, and passes on. What comes out of a man is what defiles him. From within, from the heart of a man, come evil thoughts, adulteries, murders, thefts, pride, and foolishness."

With this reply he implied that all foods are clean, the most radical heresy imaginable to the Pharisees. A basic element in the Jewish faith is that the only animals which may be eaten are those with cloven hooves that chew their cuds, and that the only fish acceptable are those with scales and fins. The great heroes of the Maccabean revolution were those Jews who chose death rather than eat pork when presented those alternatives by their Emperor Antiochus Epiphanes IV.

A further affront was offered to the religious authorities when Jesus cured a paralytic man and said to him, "Man, your sins are forgiven you." The Pharisees said, "This man speaks blasphemies. No one can forgive sin but God himself."

Whether or not he himself thought he had the power

to forgive wrong-doing, he must have known how making such a statement would be taken by the orthodox. At about this time members of his family concluded that he was unbalanced and should be taken home by force, for his own sake. They failed in their attempts to abduct him, however, and the tragedy was acted out eventually to the very end they feared.

Jesus soon put himself into a dangerous conflict with the authorities over the most basic Jewish institution, the sabbath. Jesus was taken to task by the Pharisees because his disciples plucked ears of corn to eat on the sabbath, trespassing the law against reaping on that day. Also, he healed people on the sabbath, one man with a withered hand and another with the dropsy, among others. These miraculous cures were in violation of the law which provided that a physician could treat a patient on the seventh day of the week only if the individual's life was in danger. The setting of a fractured limb is forbidden, for example, in that strict code.

When the Pharisees charged him with a disrespect for the law, he answered, "The Son of Man is lord even of the sabbath." By this reply he set himself above the most sacred law of Moses.

This direct challenge from a man attracting so many followers alarmed the Pharisees. One of their most cherished hopes is to become worthy of this promise of their god from the *Torah*: "You shall keep my sabbath and reverence my sanctuary. If you walk in my statutes and keep my commandments . . . you shall chase your enemies and they shall fall before you by the sword. Five of you shall chase a hundred, and a hundred of you shall put ten thousand to flight."

You can imagine who they have in mind.

You can also imagine how concerned they would be about this pretentious carpenter being at large, attracting proselytes, winning Jews away from compliance with what they believed to be the absolute word of their god. They saw him as a threat to their religion and to their nation.

The man made himself even more offensive by upbraiding the Pharisees who faced him, telling them they were not living up to the basic principles of Judaism. He accused them of failing to comply with the will of their god in dealings with other men. He excoriated them for proposing that they could satisfy their god and be virtuous by and through a formal compliance with a complicated code of laws. He condemned them for having allowed a moral point of view to be superseded by a legal one.

The Pharisees were sensitive to the charges Jesus made. They recognized the problem of an empty and ceremonial observance of the law, and they acknowledged the existence of some hypocrites among their number. They have preserved among their writings the words of King Alexander Jannaeus, a Sadducee, who said to his wife Alexandra from his death bed, "Do not be afraid of the Pharisees, nor of those who are not Pharisees, but fear those who are dyed to look like Pharisees..." In short, they saw their problem in this respect to be very much like that of many other religious organizations.

But who is there who likes to be accused of personal shortcomings in a public place, as Jesus was accusing those men? And he seemed to be criticizing all Pharisees along with them. The way the Galilean confronted them could lead the investigators to only one conclusion. Having adjudged his miracles genuine, they announced their decision that the man was a sorcerer. They concluded that his miracles were done with the aid of their devil.

Surely Jesus never doubted the effects his actions would have on their conclusions. He denounced them, calling them serpents and vipers. He used Pharisees in his parables as examples of self-righteous hypocrites of less virtue than common sinners. I must confess I was amused when I heard it.

He became more bold in his defiance. He declared, "I am the light of the world," thoroughly jolting their minds.

Devout Jews sought to kill him as an apostate. For example, after he had preached in his own synagogue in Nazareth, members of the congregation there, who had known him since childhood, tried to stone him and throw him over the edge of a cliff.

It was clear that, mad or sane, he knew what he was doing and understood the consequences. Before he left Galilee he predicted his crucifixion. He said to his disciples, "If any man will come after me, let him deny himself, and take up his cross and follow me."

There was a strange and mystical note that entered into his message. He foretold not only his crucifixion but his victory over death in these words: "The Son of Man must suffer many things and be rejected by the elders, the chief priests, and the scribes, and be killed, and after three days rise again."

With these words he raised the hackles of the religious hierarchy among the Jews. They found it all very reminiscent of the Babylonian belief in Tammuz that had been denounced as an abomination by Ezekiel during the captivity. If the man's intention was simply to invent a new faith, he might have taken some care to avoid elements that would be so offensive to the Jewish establishment. By choosing three days as the duration of his predicted stay in the tomb, he upset them terribly. Perhaps he didn't care.

Having cast his gage down before the leaders of his people, he turned his steps toward Jerusalem, a dreamer setting forth with his little band of disciples on the road to the one city in which, under Jewish law, he could be tried and executed for heresy.

So it was that he entered my domain and became my responsibility.

No One Ever Spoke Like Him

Along with a crowd of other pilgrims, Jesus arrived in Jerusalem at harvest time for the Feast of the Tabernacles. His entry was of great general interest among the throngs streaming into the city. He was being called a false prophet, an apostate, a blasphemer, a man possessed by a demon. He was also being called the messiah. I set men to keep close track of him.

He went up to the Temple to preach his message of salvation through love of god and man in the courts there. He was an impressive, magnetic fellow. Crowds gathered to hear him out of curiosity and listened with interest to all that he said. His presence caused the religious authorities to be very much on edge.

They cast about for ways to discredit him in the eyes of the multitude. On the seventh night of the feast, a group of scribes and Pharisees brought before Jesus a woman who had been apprehended in the act of adultery. In an effort to try to entrap him they put this question to him: "The law of Moses commands us that a woman taken in adultery must be stoned. What do you say?"

They cited a true statement of their law on the subject, the very word of their god to them. The question constituted a snare for him because the power to inflict the death penalty without the approval of the governor had been recently taken away from the Jews. I need not remind you that adultery normally is not a capital offense under Roman law.

The carpenter was placed in an awkward position. If he had said that the woman should not be stoned, his pious opponents could have charged him with contradicting the word of their god. This would have discredited him as a prophet of their god. If, on the other hand, he had said she should be stoned it would have been done forthwith. Then he would have found himself in violation of Roman law as a party to a wrongful death. He would have been in a perilous situation.

In his answer he showed both wit and wisdom. I understand he stooped and wrote in the dust of the temple court with his finger a list of sins which may be laid at the door of most men. Then he rose up and said, "Let him who is without guilt cast the first stone." Silently the crowd dwindled away without throwing a single stone. When he chose, Jesus of Nazareth could be a very intimidating man, capable of arousing feelings of self-consciousness even in men not used to the emotion, as I was to find later.

This event intensified the determination of the Pharisees to deal with him appropriately. They had been made to look foolish, which is damaging to any authorities, especially religious ones. Also, they believe that the wrath of their god will be drawn down upon the Jewish people if they fail to punish transgressors as their law requires. To do so is a part of their covenant with god.

It is a position Jewish leaders must take in order to be credible, regardless of the laws of Rome. By standing in the way of the stoning of that woman, Jesus impaired his reputation with some devout Jews.

He continued to preach in the Temple courts. Common people began to say, "Isn't this the man they seek to kill? Yet here he is speaking openly and they say nothing to him. Can it be that they know he is the Christ?"

At about this time the chief priests and the scribes sent officers to arrest him. They came back empty-handed, saying, "No one ever spoke like this man."

The fellow continued to bid defiance to both the Sadducees and Pharisees. Once again he said, "I am the light of the world." They should have been amused by such grandiloquent bravado, as a Greek or a Roman would be. If the carpenter believed himself, he was quite mad and deserved only their sympathy or at worst their laughter. But, being Jews in this day and age, they could neither sympathize nor smile.

Imagine their outrage when this poor fellow whom they had dignified with their solemn disapproval, accused them of being children of the devil when they confronted him in the Temple. They replied by telling him he was a Samaritan and was possessed by a demon.

Then Jesus referred to Abraham, the patriarch, and said that the ancient father of their race was glad to see his day had come.

They answered him, "You are not yet fifty years old, and have you seen Abraham?"

The carpenter replied impressively, "Before Abraham was, *I am*."

Now these words *I am* and *I am He* have a tremendous significance in the Jewish religion. I shall discuss the matter later in connection with the appearance of Jesus at the inquest held in the palace of the high priest after his arrest. Suffice to say here that they are found in scriptures on the lips of their god alone.

With this reply the man made a clear statement that he held himself to be one with their one god. Horrified by such heresy his questioners picked up rocks to stone him, but he managed to escape from them.

A short time later, in the Portico of Solomon in the Temple, he said, "I and the Father are one." Again his indignant opponents attempted to stone him. Again he escaped from them.

The Great Sanhedrin decided to take an official step. They called a man to appear who had been blind from birth, according to his own account, one whom the carpenter allegedly had made to see upon the sabbath day.

The Sanhedrists did not believe the man had ever been blind, and they said of Jesus, "This man is not from God, for he does not keep the sabbath."

The man who was purported to have been blind was full of praise for the carpenter and swore he was a prophet. He said, "God does not listen to sinners, but if anyone is a worshipper of God and does his will, God listens to him. If this man were not from God, he could do nothing."

For this they excommunicated the erstwhile blind man, putting all Jews on notice that there would be serious consequences to those who chose to follow the Galilean.

For a brief time, Jesus continued to move about Judea as a wandering evangelist. To those who did not understand his designs and purposes, it seemed that he was fleeing from the very death he had predicted for himself. Naturally his claims of divinity raised more and more danger for him. He was stoned in Lydda, but escaped with his life. To decrease the peril he faced, he withdrew beyond the Jordan River to Perea where he was again within the domain of Herod Antipas. From the earliest days of his ministry Jesus apparently thought he had nothing to fear from the tetrarch, who, although a shade uneasy about the carpenter, seemed to be intrigued by the stories about the miracles he worked.

Jesus preached to crowds there in Perea. Certain Pharisees, probably thinking to create problems for him with Herod Antipas similar to those that had proved fatal to John the Baptist, asked him, "Is it lawful for a man to put away his wife?" They cited the law of Moses permitting divorce. I presume they knew he had expressed himself in the past on the subject and that he preferred more recent Jewish authorities who rejected divorce. He said, "Any man who puts away his wife, and marries again, commits adultery."

Everyone was curious to see what the royal response would be to that. Ultimately time proved that the tetrarch was not troubled by Jesus' position in this controversy. Herod seemed content in the matter of his divorce to rest it upon the authority of Moses. No one knew how Herodias would react, but apparently even she was not prepared to suggest that Herod lock up any of his subjects for condemning divorce, as long as they didn't mention hers specifically.

Some of the Pharisees came to Jesus and told him he should flee from Perea because Herod sought to take his life. His answer betrayed an old contempt for the tetrarch. "Go and tell that fox . . ." he said, "it cannot be that a prophet should perish out of Jerusalem."

The motives of those Pharisees are not known to me. It may be that they actually did fear for his life, or it may be that they wanted to induce him to leave the lands ruled by his own monarch and return to Judea, into the jurisdiction of the Great Sanhedrin.

In any case, his contempt of Herod showed that he felt he was in no danger in Perea. When I sent Jesus to appear before Herod in Jerusalem the day he died, the tetrarch showed an unwillingness to do anything to punish the man, which confirmed the judgment of Jesus concerning him. On the other hand, it is apparent that Jesus believed that if he were to return to Jerusalem, which he referred to as the city that kills the prophets, it would be to go to his grave.

Then it was that there occurred an event which set everything in motion toward the final resolution of the affair. While Jesus lingered east of the Jordan River, a friend of his named Lazarus fell ill. The carpenter had often stayed with this man and his two sisters in the town of Bethany on the south-eastern slope of the Mount of Olives. Lazarus's sisters sent word to ask Jesus to come and heal him, but he hesitated in returning.

When at last he set foot on the road from Perea to Jericho and Jerusalem it was too late to cure Lazarus of his illness. According to the accounts I heard, the man had been in his tomb four days by the time Jesus walked into Bethany.

On hearing of the death of his friend, the carpenter reportedly went to the cave where Lazarus was buried and called on him to come forth. And he did. Whether this was an elaborate trick, as some of my more worldly subordinates concluded, or whether Lazarus had been in a cataleptic state and was awakened by Jesus, the effect was all the same. A great many Jews accepted the resurrection of Lazarus as genuine. The Pharisees generally concluded that it was another manifestation by the carpenter of either black magic or pure deception. The proselytes of Jesus hailed it as a great miracle done by the hand of their god.

Word came to me in Caesarea that all of Jerusalem

was talking about the event. In every inn in the city, it seemed, people were arguing over whether Jesus of Nazareth was a prophet of god or a priest of the devil. All of the feelings about the resurrection of the dead being the sign of the advent of the messiah, which accompanied the raising of the daughter of Jairus and the son of the widow of Nain, were revived and intensified. The raising of Lazarus probably sealed Jesus's fate, because previously he had been a cause of concern only to the Pharisees. Now he had become a source of worry to the Sadducees, who are very practical politicians.

Hopeful mobs of people went flocking to see Jesus, according to the commander of the cohort at the Fortress Antonia. They had been looking for a worker of wonders, and one had come at last. Some of the stories about his birth were being circulated. The Jewish authorities reported that they feared the mobs might become uncontrollable. They recalled how Jesus had once been offered a crown after the affair of the loaves and fishes. They were apprehensive that some agitator of revolutionary sympathies might make the same gesture again, and that the hour had come that he might be ready to accept it. Times had changed, too. Now that he had made the mighty proclamation, "I am He," it seemed he might be ready for the role of messiah.

Public enthusiasm could force him either to accept leadership or be rejected by the people. In his conflict with the religious authorities, the multitude could give him victory and life. The Jewish hierarchy feared that might happen, as well as the fact that for him to accept leadership would be to set the wheels of rebellion in motion. That was what so many zealots among the Jews were waiting for someone to do.

The priesthood was full of old men who remembered the thousands of crosses around the walls of Jerusalem set up by Varus in the course of the last insurrection. They remembered the tragedy of Sepphoris and a number of other futile outbreaks in recent years. They feared that Rome will only tolerate a limited number of rebellions before it concludes that a people is so intractable that it must be destroyed as a nation, reduced and dispersed in the way the Assyrians dealt with the ten northern tribes of Israel.

Responsible Jews knew that theirs was a nation which by then had tested the patience of Rome so many times that they were coming to the brink of the abyss.

For that reason a council of the chief priests and Pharisees was convened to discuss the emergency. The question presented to the assembly was this: "What shall we do? This man does many miracles. If we leave him alone everyone will believe in him, and the Romans will come and take away our place and our nation." The emphasis was on the concerns of the Sadducees rather than on those of the Pharisees. The latter had long since decided that the man was a menace to the nation for spiritual reasons, but they seemed to play a subordinate role in these deliberations. What they would have done if the matter had been left up to them alone is not clear to me.

Joseph ben Caiaphas, the High Priest, expressed the opinion that became the conclusion of the council when he said, "It is expedient that one man should die for the people, that the Nation should not perish."

The Great Sanhedrin had previously ordered his arrest and sent its officers to apprehend him, but it had not been possible to take him into custody because of his popularity with his listeners and because he had overawed the men sent to arrest him. Now, following the leadership of Caiaphas, the high priests and elders took counsel together to put him to death. They ordered that, if any man knew the place where Jesus was, he should reveal it, in order that they might take him.

It becomes clear, in looking back over what he had said on various occasions, that Jesus of Nazareth was preparing himself to die in Jerusalem. Presumably this attitude was related to John the Baptist having called him "The Lamb of God that taketh away the sins of the world." The Christians consider his crucifixion a blood sacrifice in accordance with the requirements of Jewish law for the expiation of sins.

While he had come to accept the thought of death for himself, he seemed to have his own ideas about when it should take place. Apparently for symbolic reasons, he chose to postpone it until Passover, when Jewish men lead lambs into the Temple to be sacrificed, to provide the main course for each of their families for the feast of unleavened bread. Therefore he retreated into Samaria until that time had come.

At last he turned his steps toward Jerusalem for the last time. When he returned he stayed again in Bethany, as was his custom. It was at the beginning of Passover Week. There was a thrill of excitement among the throngs in the city. He had supper at the home of Lazarus and his two sisters. In the evening an army of pilgrims and residents of Jerusalem trooped out from the city to see them.

Everyone knew that something final was about to happen. Either the religious authorities would retreat before the carpenter or they would kill him. His enemies wondered if he would save himself by accepting the messianic crown of rebellion. So did his friends.

And so did I.

Triumph and Despair

On the first day of the week Jesus of Nazareth entered the gates of Jerusalem for the last time. He came over the shoulder of the Mount of Olives from Bethany in the afternoon, riding on a donkey colt. It seemed as though he was designing the close of his life to conform to ancient prophecy regarding the messiah, as the beginning had done.

The Jews have a tradition which says the messiah will appear on that hill when he comes, and their prophet Zechariah wrote long ago, "Tell the daughters of Zion, behold, thy king cometh unto thee: he is just and having salvation; lowly and riding upon an ass, and upon a colt, the foal of an ass."

It was an imperial gesture, clearly stating his claims and inviting Jews to greet him as their savior. He was offering a colossal affront to the Pharisees and Sadducees who had pronounced him a heretic, and had ordered his arrest.

Masses of pilgrims and residents of Jerusalem went

out to hail him as their king. A multitude issued from the eastern gates of the city, across the valley of the brook Kidron. They hurried up the hill through the groves of olive trees to meet him on the mountain. They were bearing palm fronds, as though to welcome royalty. They laid in his path green branches they had torn from trees, and strewed their garments before him. According to the reports I heard, he seemed to have all of the self assurance of Caesar Augustus himself.

A procession followed him into the city shouting *Hosannah*, which means *God Save Us*. As they passed through the gates they cried, "Blessed is he that cometh in the name of the Lord," and, "This is the prophet Jesus of Nazareth from Galilee," and "Hosannah in the highest. Hosannah to the Son of David."

Word of that triumphal scene reached me in the Praetorium in Jerusalem where I was staying to observe events during the holiday season. It was a reminder that many people will take a man for what he believes himself to be. One man's delusions too often become another man's faith.

As he passed through the streets it was as the King of the Jews, with all of the deference and acclaim due a king. Pharisees among that tumult thought they were seeing their worst fears being realized. They knew I was watching, and must have wondered if I would order the garrison out of the Antonia Fortress to cut down that boisterous mob. Only a short time before that I had sent troops into the Temple to cut down a wild rabble of Galileans. The Jews poetically expressed their feelings by saying that I mixed their blood with that of their sacrifices. Concerned for the lives of the demonstrators, the Pharisees called upon the carpenter to rebuke them.

He answered them, "I tell you that if these men were silent the very stones would cry out."

It seemed to me a curious thing for him to accept the adulation of that would-be army of rebellion. He made it clear both before and after that he had no desire to be the kind of leader they were looking for.

Perhaps he felt the acclaim was due him for what he believed himself to be. Perhaps that triumphal procession seemed appropriate to him as a sign to the nation that he actually was the messiah promised by the prophets, the Son of Man through whom the kingdom of their god is to be fulfilled.

Because it was evening when he entered Jerusalem in his moment of triumph, he stayed in the city only briefly. He visited the Temple courts, which were quiet at that hour. Then he went back over the mountain to Bethany with his disciples, to spend the night there. Like him, I relaxed and went to bed.

The following morning he returned to the city and the Temple, a very busy place at that season. The majestic courts King Herod built were full of the lowing of cattle, the bleating of lambs, and the cooing of doves in their cages, all waiting to be sold and slaughtered. There was the bicker of business and the chinking of coins. The money changers who accepted foreign coin and gave Jewish money in return for use as offerings were busy. (This service was provided because foreign money could not be offered to the service of their god. Offerings had to be made in Jewish money which bore no images or likenesses of any living thing.) In the background could be heard endless incantations over the sacrifices on the bloody altar, and the sounds of the cymbal, psalter, and trumpet, as well as the chanting of the Levites and the prayers of the faithful.

Striding into this busy exchange, the carpenter made

chaos out of disorder. With a scourge he had fashioned out of cords, he began to drive out those who bought and sold there. He overturned the tables of the money changers and the seats of the merchants.

Full of righteous anger he cried, "Isn't it written, 'My house shall be called a house of prayer?' But you have made it a den of thieves."

Once again he had aggressively confronted the religious hierarchy in a way that left them no retreat. Those men transacting business in the Temple courts were a source of income for the chief priests, who sold the licenses to trade there. The traders were called "the sons of Annas," after the former High Priest whose family still remained in control of that office through the person of his son-in-law Caiaphas.

The fact that the chief priests sanctioned trade in the holy Temple of the Jews was generally considered to be to their discredit. I heard that a reform movement at last put an end to trading in those courts only a year or two ago, so all that business today is transacted outside the Temple. It must be a quiet place now, quite unlike what it was.

Thirty years ago, however, that action of Jesus was a daring challenge to the prerogatives of the priests. It was a bold assertion of his own authority, a powerful move because most Jews already felt that the doing of business in the Temple was an abuse. The multitude of Greek, Egyptian, Babylonian, Parthian, and Palestinian Jews in the city was well pleased with their new hero I was informed.

Each one of his actions alarmed the Pharisees and Sadducees more than the last. They continued to confer on the emergency to find a way to deal with it.

Jesus went daily to teach in the courts of the Temple. The temper of the crowd there was such that it remained impossible for the officers of the Sanhedrin to lay their hands upon him. The fears and frustrations of the hierarchy were renewed hourly. Time after time they challenged him there, engaging him in controversy, thinking to contrast their scholarly learning in the law with the ordinary knowledge of a tradesman. By this tactic they hoped to reduce the esteem of the multitude for him. Day after day he confounded them with wise and clever replies.

At last they devised a question to entrap him that was a forensic masterpiece. They confronted him in his usual place and asked, "Tell us what you think. Is it or is it not lawful to pay tribute to Caesar?"

If he answered that Jews should not pay taxes due the Emperor, he would be espousing the cause of revolution. The rebellions of Judas of Galilee had been against the imposition of Roman taxes, which remained the most likely stimulus for a new revolt. Many in crowds who hailed him as their king on the first day of the week were looking to him to lead that rebellion. Naturally, if he had said that Jews should not pay taxes to Caesar, I would have him arrested and executed for inciting the people to rebellion. It would have been a plain case of *laese maiestas*.

If, on the other hand, he replied that the Jews should pay their taxes, he would lose some of the public support which had protected him from arrest. He would be in the position of recommending submission to Roman rule; and many of his rowdy followers would abandon the hope that he might be their messiah.

The trap was so well laid he could not escape it. He had a choice between only two answers. He was as clever as ever, but the guile of Ulysses himself would have availed him little.

Remembering the ruin of Sepphoris, no doubt, and knowing the disaster which would flow from any new rebellion, he counseled the Jews to pay their taxes. He did it in an interesting way. He asked the Pharisees who had put the question to show him a denarius. They did so. He asked, "Whose likeness and inscription is this?" They replied, "Caesar's." He then said, "Render unto Caesar the things that are Caesar's, and unto God the things that are God's."

What he did was very wily. He asked them to show him a denarius, a Roman coin, legal tender for the payment of the tax. They could hardly refuse, even if they could have anticipated his reply, which was not likely. Of course, Roman money cannot be given to the Jewish god, because of the images upon it. I was entertained by the way he disposed of his scholarly opponents. The general populace seemed to be impressed, and thought his response quite profound. In reflecting upon it, I suppose it was.

Yet he could not avoid alienating support he could not afford to lose. It was assumed he was saying that Rome was providing peace and order and justice, and that it was proper to pay the price for it. Generally, his answer was taken to be a call for obedience to authority. He was sounding better and better to me, but worse and worse to the zealots whose support the Pharisees sought to win away from him.

There were a few more exchanges in the temple. The Pharisees asked him which is the greatest commandment and which is the second. As good politicians they were simply raising various questions by then to see if their opponent would reveal some odd opinion or another which would discredit him in the eyes of the faithful. Responding to this inquiry he gave the same answer that they themselves would have given if asked. He said that a man should love god above all. After that he should love his fellow man as much as himself. Not only was this a basic doctrine of Judaism, it was also the sum and substance of the message he had been preaching from the earliest days in the fields of Galilee. This answer was another indication that, however much the man may have been a threat to religious orthodoxy, he constituted no problem for civil government.

Then he launched into a last denunciation of his enemies, a Philippic in which Cicero himself might have taken pride. Let me offer as an example of Jesus's oratorical art a few lines from it, as they are given in the collections of notes preserved by the Christians.

He said "Woe unto you, scribes, Pharisees, hypocrites, for you compass the sea and the land to make one proselyte, and when he is made, you make him twice as fit for hell as you are yourselves. Woe unto you, scribes, Pharisees, hypocrites, for you pay the tithe of mint and anise and cumin, and have omitted the weightier matters of the law, judgment, mercy, and faith.

"Woe unto you, scribes, Pharisees, hypocrites, for you are like whited sepulchres, which appear beautiful outwardly, but are full of dead men's bones and uncleanness. Even so you appear righteous unto men, but within you are full of hypocrisy and iniquity."

He concluded with another challenge.

"Woe unto you, scribes, Pharisees, hypocrites, because you build monuments to the prophets and decorate the graves of the righteous men you destroyed, and say, 'If we had lived in the days of our fathers we would not have joined them in killing the prophets.' Wherefore be witnesses unto yourselves that you are the children of them that killed the prophets. Live up to the example they set for you."

It was with this final defiant cry to the Pharisees that he closed his public ministry.

As he withdrew from the Temple with his disciples, they called to his attention the beauty and grandeur of that majestic building. He said to them, "I tell you there shall not be left here one stone upon another which shall not be thrown down."

To those of us who have lived in the shadow of that tremendous structure, it seemed an incredible thought. Yet it is not so unthinkable today, with all the rumblings of sedition in Palestine.

Jesus recognized in the tumultuous welcome he had been accorded two days before the suicidal inclination of the Jews to run toward the brink of the abyss. He was prophesying that in time others like Judas of Galilee would arise and the Jews would receive them as he had been received himself. He must have been thinking back on the days when, as a child, he had walked with his parents through the desolation that had once been the great city of Sepphoris.

On that day as he left Jerusalem, he was predicting rebellion and tragedy. He may yet prove to be a true prophet, at least in this respect, the way things are going in Palestine.

A little later, on the road back over the Mount of Olives, he said, "Heaven and earth will pass away, but my words will not pass away," putting himself back into his proper perspective as a poor mad fellow confident that what he said would echo down the corridors of time.

On the first day of Passover week there occurred his triumphal entry into the city. On the second he drove the merchants out of the temple courts. On the third he denounced the scribes and Pharisees. Each day he applied new pressure on the authorities. The thought of this going on very long was intolerable to them.

The hierarchy met in the palace of Caiaphas to see how they might take him by stealth in some private place. His support among various elements of the populace still remained too broad for them to want to try to arrest him in public as Jewish law required. There might be disorder and bloodshed, and he might escape, if they followed the normal procedures.

Fortuitously for them, one of the twelve favorite disciples of Jesus presented himself to them and asked them what they would give him to deliver the carpenter into their hands. They promised to pay him thirty pieces of silver. Offering that particular sum of money turned out to be a blunder.

Thirty pieces of silver was the traditional price for a slave. It had been so understood in times past when their prophet Zechariah put into the mouth of their god the words, "... so they weighed for my price thirty pieces of silver."

The authorities were aware of the fact that the carpenter seemed to be consciously taking steps to make his life conform to the prophecies about the messiah, and they were offended by it. Yet, even if the man had arranged to consummate every scripture he could, it was beyond his power to do anything about this one. So they did it for him.

Perhaps there was an ironic humor in it that appealed to them. They may have considered their contriving this to be an expression of their opinion about his arranging to ride down from the Mount of Olives on the colt of an ass. It may be that they thought it was a way to ridicule the fellow's claims. It proved to be so serious a mistake in so short a time that they never discussed publicly their reasons for the gesture. It ranked with Herod's massacre of the infants of Bethlehem as a thoughtless act which helped build the legend. If all of the fulfillments of prophecy in the carpenter's life had depended on his own actions and those of Mary and Joseph, there would be very few Christians today.

When the bargain was made with Judas the last act of the drama commenced.

The reason Judas betrayed the master he had followed

so long has come to interest both the Jews and the Christians. Did he lose faith in Jesus and act in accordance with Jewish law to deliver up the deceiver of the people to destruction? Or had he just given up his hopes for the establishment of a Jewish state by Jesus as a messianic king? Had the hope of a high place in that kingdom been his motivation for following the carpenter from the beginning? Having lost this hope of advancement, did he decide to make the best of a bad bargain, and get out of a disappointing experience with a little money at least to show for three misspent years? No one knows.

Some Christians cannot believe that anyone who was exposed to their Christ, as Judas was, could ever lose faith in him. They think that Judas was convinced by the wonders he had seen that the Galilean was the true son of a god, who could deliver himself from the power of the authorities by calling upon his god to intervene. They feel that Judas wanted to precipitate events and expedite the establishment of their god's kingdom on earth. They believe that he saw himself as the instrument of god's will.

However, the prevailing opinion among Christians, as far as I can determine, is that their devil took possession of Judas and used him for his own purposes. Although if that is the case, I don't credit their devil with much foresight.

On his last night on earth Jesus of Nazareth had supper in Jerusalem with his twelve apostles. This event is often referred to among the Christians. Apparently having gotten wind of what was afoot, he told them that one of them would betray him. The story Christians tell about this is rather touching because each of the twelve, concerned that it might be himself who would do it, asked, "Is it I?" Each of them, except Judas, could only imagine that the betrayal would be inadvertent, and each wanted either reassurance or a warning, in order that he might take care to avoid such an awful responsibility. Before they finished eating, Jesus indicated to one or two that it would be Judas, but he did not let them know that it would be a willful act. If he had done so, they surely would have done everything they could to persuade him to avoid his usual retreats, where Judas could find him.

They say the carpenter privately told Judas that he knew of his purposes and said to him, "What you are going to do, do quickly." Then he sent the man on his way.

I have already referred to the ideas that caused that strange man to accept death as he did, but I should like to offer here his own summation of his thoughts on the subject. He once said in this connection, "Unless a grain of wheat falls to the earth and dies it remains alone; but if it dies, it bears much fruit." It was all very poetic.

This last supper of Jesus of Nazareth was a transcendental affair. He declared that the bread was his flesh and the wine his blood, and that they should re-enact the ceremony in his memory, after his death. I shouldn't be surprised if it were the repetition of this mystical rite that has given rise to the tales about the Christians drinking blood in their worship services, stories that have revolted the Roman people.

The notes that have been compiled about what he said to his disciples after supper are quite beautiful. They describe a last farewell to eleven friends who loved him as few men are ever loved, and to one who betrayed him as many men are betrayed. In part he said, "Let not your heart be troubled. You believe in God, believe also in me. In my father's house are many mansions. I go to prepare a place for you; and if I go to prepare a place for you I will come again and receive you unto myself, that where I am you may be also.

"In a little while the world will see me no more. Peace

I leave with you, my peace I give unto you. So that the world may know I love the father, and as the father has given me direction, even so will I do as he commands ...

"A new commandment I give unto you, that you love one another, even as I have loved you ...

"Arise, let us go hence."

I believe he could still have lived, had he so chosen. He could have gone to Bethany that night and stayed with his friends there. Or he might have hidden himself in any one of a thousand places around the city till morning. He was probably still safe from arrest in the streets during daylight hours. When morning came he could have escaped with a company of friends down the road through Jericho. Being an active man he could have been across the Jordan River by nightfall. There he would have been within the jurisdiction of Herod Antipas, where he had always been safe in times past.

But that was not his purpose. Having decided it was his destiny to die for mankind, he went just across the brook Kidron to a place called *Gethsemane*, which means *oil press*. It is an olive orchard of considerable extent at the base of the Mount of Olives.

The garden of Gethsemane is a place that Judas knew him to frequent. Jesus stayed there, praying they say, until Judas came leading a band of officers and soldiers.

Judas identified his friend to them with a kiss. There was a little skirmish. After Peter slashed one of the men with his sword, Jesus told his disciples not to resist. He allowed himself to be led quietly away toward the battlements of the dark city.

The Affairs of Men

Jesus Christ was brought before me to be tried for treason shortly before my own world was turned upside down by the death of Lucius Aelius Sejanus. It was in October of the following year that Tiberius Caesar, burdened with age and infirmities, appeared in the Senate to denounce his chief prefect as a traitor and to demand his death, much to the astonishment and pleasure of the Senators.

Prior to the execution of Sejanus and his family and friends, which I was fortunate enough to escape, the government of Rome was still in good order, to all appearances. The strains in the structure of government that were developing could still be overlooked by those who preferred to do so. By then the Emperor was failing badly, but he still had a friend he could trust to rule the world in his name.

No one then foresaw the disarray into which the Imperial Government would fall as a result of Tiberius Caesar's decision to believe the accusations against the man who had been his ears and his voice for so long.

The enemies of Sejanus hoped to pull him down and set up one of themselves in his place. It could not be. Grown old and disillusioned, the Emperor never trusted anyone else until the day he died; and considering how he at last was ushered out of this world, it turned out that he was quite right to be fearful.

At the time of the trial of Jesus of Nazareth, the Emperor was at Capri, whither he had retreated to his private pursuits so many years before. Sejanus was the government. The Praetorian guard kept order in Rome and, at times, in the Senate as well.

Sejanus was hated by the patricians for the power he held over them. The Empire was full of his enemies, mostly men of high birth and position. Rome fumed with conspiracy and intrigue against him. My own situation was affected because I represented Sejanus in Palestine. Although Sejanus was yet to fall to ruin, the destruction of status quo was desired and foreseen by many.

In Galilee and Perea, old Herod Antipas still ruled on as tetrarch, as he had done for thirty years and more. He had tried to enhance his reputation by rebuilding Sepphoris on a grander scale, but it only reminded his subjects of the destruction and misery worked upon the old city on his behalf by the Roman army. In time he overshadowed this great project with another, when he erected his beautiful new capital city on the shores of the Sea of Galilee. He called it Tiberias, as a tribute to Tiberius Caesar, and he caused the lake to be renamed the Lake of Tiberias, also in honor of the Emperor. As I mentioned earlier, the new city was built in part upon a cemetery. Devout Jews will not enter upon ground which has been defiled by the dead, so they wouldn't go into the new capital. Herod also arranged for his palace there to be embellished with all manner of ornamentation, which violated Jewish laws forbidding the making of graven images. Herod Antipas had been raised to manhood in the Hellenistic court of Herod the Great. In the building of his palace at Tiberias he showed that he was no more interested in making religious orthodoxy a policy of his government than his father had been.

Like all of the other Herods, he was a great builder. Like all of the other Herods, he gained no credit among his people with his costly monuments. Good Jews disapproved of Tiberias as an indication that their ruler lacked proper respect for the law. They disliked the idea of a Jewish capital city and royal palace which no good Jew would enter. It was a sign that the government of Galilee was one made up of impious men and gentiles.

Herod's throne had been shaken by other events. His first wife had been the daughter of Aretas, the King of the Nabateans. He put her aside to marry Herodias, who was his niece as well as his brother's wife. This marriage was contrary to the law of the Jews on both counts, and brought him further discredit as an ungodly man unworthy to rule god's people.

His angry father-in-law, King Aretas, began to make threatening moves. The impending war and the misery it would entail also aroused popular feeling against Herod Antipas. Subsequently the war was fought and ended in defeat for the tetrarch. Many Jewish subjects considered this disaster a just punishment for Herod's various sins, including the murder of John the Baptist. By those who thought John to have been a prophet of god, his execution was considered one of the greatest impieties of the ruler of Galilee and Perea.

Herod Antipas was an Epicurean. He was not given to strong beliefs. He avoided conflicts except where his comfort, pleasure, or convenience were involved. With care and with guile he survived as a friend of Rome, so he could enjoy life as it came to him.

The safety of Jesus of Nazareth was never threatened

by Herod Antipas. The tetrarch did not have to enter into the new religious controversy raised by the carpenter, and he chose not to. When he locked up John the Baptist, it was because he felt John might so arouse his followers that they might attempt to establish the new kingdom he preached, but the impetus to kill the prophet came from Herodias, the queen, who was infuriated by John's denunciations of their unlawful marriage. Herod had not wished to execute John. He was aware of the political problems that killing the prophet would arouse. He considered John to be a righteous man, but he found himself trapped into beheading the Baptist by the wiles of Herodias.

Like most men, Herod Antipas seemed to be more interested in miracles than in gods. He was intrigued by the stories he heard about the carpenter from Nazareth. The tetrarch wondered if Jesus were not John the Baptist brought back to earth as a worker of wonders. He showed no antipathy toward the supposed reincarnation of John. Instead he expressed the desire to see him, but Jesus would not come to court and satisfy the friendly curiosity of his monarch. Being a very devout Jewish man, Jesus would not enter Tiberias. It may also be that he wanted to avoid a situation where he might be called on to comment upon the marriage of the tetrarch to Queen Herodias, as his cousin had done.

The tetrarch did not wish to repeat the error he had made in the case of John the Baptist, and since Herodias had nothing against Jesus, he remained safe in Galilee and Perea.

As a final note to close the story of Herod Antipas, ten years after the death of Jesus the tetrarch made a serious mistake. At the urging of his wife, he went to Rome to ask Caligula to be raised to the rank of king, an honor which had been granted to his nephew Herod Agrippa, when the young man succeeded his father as the ruler of Iturea and Trachonitis. Agrippa had succeeded in wheedling the more royal title out of the Emperor because they were close friends. In fact Herod Agrippa had been raised in Rome as a childhood companion of Claudius Caesar, and had seen Caligula grow up, almost as a member of the family. Agrippa used this friendship well. He sent word to Caligula that his uncle was conspiring with foreign enemies against Rome. Instead of receiving further honors from Caesar, Antipas lost all of his dominions to Herod Agrippa, who became the ruler of all of Palestine and briefly restored the kingdom of the Jews for the last time.

Herod Antipas, by order of Caligula, was banished to Lugdunum in Gaul, where he remained until he died. His wife Herodias remained at the old man's side throughout those years of exile. Surprisingly enough, theirs turned out to be a story of true love, in an age when such stories are becoming rare.

At the time Jesus came to trial my own situation as governor was difficult. Direct Roman rule had been reestablished almost twenty years before, when Augustus Caesar deposed Archelaus in response to petitions from the leading men of Judea. At last the time had come when the Jews were beginning to become restive under Roman rule, which they had expected to be temporary when they requested it.

My immediate predecessor was Valerius Gratus, who ruled for eleven relatively uneventful years. Governors of Judea, Samaria, and Idumea in those days held the rank of *prefect*. It was not till after the time of King Herod Agrippa that the post was raised to the level of *procurator*.

Governors there have the power to choose the High Priests of Judaism. It is a power important in controlling the Jews because of the great authority of the office. The High Priests are appointed for only one year at a time, which keeps them on a tight rein. Gratus dismissed the powerful Annas from the office, but the influence of Annas was restored soon after, when his faction reached an understanding with the Governor. Eleazar, his son, was designated High Priest. Subsequently Gratus elevated Joseph ben Caiaphas, the son-in-law of Annas, to hold the office.

Throughout my ten years there I re-appointed Caiaphas annually. He served a total of eighteen years, far longer than any other man since the destruction of the Hasmonean dynasty of priest-kings. A few months after Vitellius, who was then President of Syria, removed me as Governor, he completed the change in government by replacing Caiaphas as High Priest as well.

The understanding between Caiaphas and myself was mutually beneficial. With Annas he had great authority which was used to maintain stability and order in the province. Roman rule and the peace depended upon the effective cooperation of the Governor and the High Priest. Caiaphas and I were useful to each other.

I had need of his help. Like most men in positions of power, I faced various problems. To begin with, I had become Governor because I was a loyal friend and supporter of Sejanus, and he was the most unpopular man in Judea since Antiochus Epiphanes tried to make them eat pork, two centuries before.

It was seven years before my appointment that Sejanus had moved to diminish the special privileges granted by Julius Caesar and Caesar Augustus to the Jews throughout the Empire. He considered them to be a potentially disruptive minority because they are determined to maintain their distinct identity. Over the years other subject peoples have been gradually giving up their peculiar customs and religions under the tolerant aegis of Rome. All but the Jews have been by degrees becoming easier subjects of the Empire. Like Antiochus

Epiphanes, Sejanus concluded that there might be no end to the trouble that would flow from leaving their religion undisturbed. Unlike Antiochus, whose attempts to stamp out their idiosyncracies were tinged with irrationality born of anger, Sejanus was simply trying to pursue a sound public policy. Considering the misunderstanding and hostility that have killed so many Jews in Alexandria and elsewhere in recent years, it appears that only by assimilation with the peoples around them will the Jews escape destruction in a century or two. Their god will have to be very active on their behalf to preserve them longer than that.

Of course the Emperor Tiberius, after the fall of Sejanus, restored the old privileges of the Jews. This was accompanied by a renewal of all of the old resentments that every other people feels about those privileges. The ultimate consequences are yet to be seen.

When I came to power, I hoped to bring a degree of peace to that troubled land I had been given to rule. With the support of Sejanus, I chose to govern with a strong hand. I believe that it is necessary to achieve an orderly submission among the Jews. I am satisfied that Nebuchadnezzar, Sargon, and Antiochus Epiphanes were correct in concluding that this difficult people must be required to acknowledge authority or they will resist it, even though the measures those old despots employed were inappropriate in my day and age.

I was appointed prefect of Judea, Samaria, and Idumea in the twelfth year of the reign of Tiberius Caesar. In Rome Sejanus was Tiberius. In Palestine I was Sejanus.

Early in my time in office I chose to manifest to the Jews the authority of Caesar. When the time came to remove the headquarters of the army from Caesarea, the capital, to the ancient city of Jerusalem for the winter, I took the opportunity to declare my policy.

I issued orders that the legions carry their usual standards bearing likenesses of Tiberius Caesar. It was after nightfall when the troops entered the city, so there was no outcry. In the morning the soldiers proceeded to pay honor to their standards as images of the god-emperor, in accordance with the custom throughout the Empire. Because of the abhorrence of the Jews for graven images of any sort, Roman legions had previously carried into Jerusalem only those ensigns which bore no such devices.

The Jews had always maintained that it would be offensive to their god, whom they believe to be present there in the Temple, to bring effigies into their holy city. Therefore they were in a turmoil in the morning.

Certainly it is an affront to Caesar that his face not be allowed to be shown in one of his cities. It therefore seemed to me to be a healthy gesture to terminate this special treatment of the Jews. Only by treating them like other people will we ever convince them they are like other people.

I was resolved to stand by what I felt to be a sound decision when, as I anticipated, crowds of Jews came down to Caesarea to petition me to remove the standards.

I listened to their entreaties for five days, sitting in a judgment seat in the city square. I explained many times at length how such a step would tend to injure Caesar. Often as I listened to the clamor that week I reflected on the words of Cicero that the Jews are a noisy and tumultuous people. Each day I expected the crowd to diminish and the importunings to wane, but they did not.

I concluded at last that patience would not secure an abatement to the nuisance. On the sixth day I directed some of the guard to arm themselves secretly and to be ready to respond to orders. The crowd from Jerusalem continued to belabor me about the standards that day. I threatened to command my soldiers to kill them unless they stopped troubling me and agreed to return to their homes.

Those strange men threw themselves down upon the ground, laying their necks bare for the swords of the soldiers. From the ground they cried out that they would rather die than see their laws broken.

Being a rational man, I was not prepared for such a reaction. Obviously I could not order that so many men be killed. Some were prominent leaders among the Jews. The consequences would have been more grave than those which would flow from withdrawing the standards, which were quite serious enough.

I relented and ordered the standards returned to Caesarea. While I believe there was, practically speaking, no alternative for me, I often regretted the outcome of the affair. It troubled me for the remainder of my administration. I determined myself not to allow such a thing to happen again.

Another situation soon arose which affected my relationship with the Jews. The city of Jerusalem was outgrowing the available water supply. It became evident that the problem required solution, so I undertook a major public works project, the building of an aqueduct forty-two miles long to bring the waters of the Arrab River from near the city of Hebron to Jerusalem.

It was a necessary work, of essential benefit to the people of Jerusalem. It had to be built and it had to be paid for. The only funds sufficient for the task were in the treasury of the Temple, where they were kept as a sacred hoard, doing no particular good to anyone.

When I declared my intention to invest some of that money for the good of the public, tens of thousands of Jews congregated. They created a furor and demanded that I give up the project. I was reproached and reviled whenever I appeared in a public place. I decided to address this problem as I had the earlier one, but to bring it to a different conclusion.

I sent soldiers out into the crowd one day with daggers under their cloaks. They surrounded the demonstrators, whom I ordered to disperse. Instead, they redoubled their abuse of me. The time had come to set things between myself and the troublemakers in proper order. I gave the soldiers the signal to fall upon them. A great many were slain, and many more escaped only after being wounded. Thus an end was put to this seditious activity and my subjects became more respectful of my authority. However, aside from Caiaphas and the Saducees, the Jews became more zealous in their hopes to find a way to discredit me and Sejanus.

The water project was carried forward to completion. It stands as the chief landmark of my administration in Palestine. If I am remembered, it will be for that aqueduct.

In keeping with the policies of Sejanus, I took steps to discontinue another special dispensation to the Jews. In deference to their superstitions, the coins in Palestine had always born upon their faces only words and numbers. I provided for the issuance of coins bearing the likenesses of the gods, which would have the result that their own money could no more be offered to the Jewish god than foreign money could. Given patience, this change might have some beneficial effects. This, too, occasioned a howl of protest, and strengthened the resolve of many Jews to embarrass me if they could.

There were also difficulties when I mounted votive shields dedicated to Tiberius on the walls of the palace of Herod the Great, where I resided when I was in Jerusalem. But that happened after the death of Christ, so I shall not take time to relate all that took place in that connection.

Before I had been in Palestine long, the Jews began

to complain about me unceasingly, to make my position difficult, to clip my wings, in effect. A writer of some note among the Jews, named Philo of Alexandria, charges me with being stubborn — it seems odd to hear that from a Jew — and tyrannical. He accuses me of extortion and persecution of his people. He says that I dislike them. However, it is not necessary to like people to govern them well. Sometimes it is better not to.

I should like to point out that the murmuring against Roman governors, which commenced in my time there, has been increasing ever since, almost without cessation. Misunderstandings between Jewish subjects and Roman governors have become established routine. For the last few years Jewish zealots have been carrying short daggers concealed under their cloaks to assassinate friends of Rome in public places by bumping into them and surreptitiously stabbing them. No one is safe from them, and Rome has fewer and fewer friends among the Jews.

In contrast to the current tumultuous uproar now reported from Palestine by Florus, the present governor, my administration was almost tranquil.

It was not then known in Rome, however, that what was causing complaints against me was the inevitable development of resentment against Roman rule, as it became increasingly permanent, contrary to the desires of the Jews. The concomitant fact was that any Roman governor would eventually have to move in the direction I moved, for the sake of Caesar.

The light that the passage of time casts had not illuminated the judgment of men in Rome in this regard while I was prefect of Judea, Samaria, and Idumea. The revelations of the then unknown future were of no help to me in those days, as Rome received reports uncomplimentary to me. My position became more difficult with the passage of time.

There was one spectre that haunted all of the governors of eastern provinces in those days, and that was the ghost of Crassus. It had not been so many years before that the Parthians had inflicted the worst defeat in the history of the Roman army upon Crassus at Carrhae. There were a lot of old men who remembered the disorders in Palestine in the time of Herod the Great, and how the Parthians had descended on that strife-torn land to drive Herod into exile and put a puppet Hasmonean on the throne. Rome had nothing to fear from Jewish insurrection, except further Parthian intervention. That, however, was a serious threat.

As I have indicated, the religion of the Jews occupied my attention during my entire ten years in Palestine. The problems related to it sprang up like weeds in a field. It was never possible to anticipate the outcome of cutting down a few of those weeds.

For example, when I ordered the suppression of the disorderly crowd of Galilean pilgrims in the Temple, a number were killed and wounded. Various manageable difficulties ensued. However, a similar event later ruined me.

A tumult had been raised in Samaria by a self-appointed prophet. The man promised to show the Samaritans sacred objects and vessels placed by Moses on Mount Gerizim. (This has been the most holy of mountains to the Samaritans ever since the Jews rejected their assistance in rebuilding the Temple in Jerusalem, and the Samaritan king chose Mount Gerizim as the site for their temple.)

A multitude of Samaritans gathered at a village called Tirabatha to ascend their holy mountain. Many were armed and there was a messianic fervor taking hold of them.It seemed a distinct possibility that the fellow might have planted some counterfeit relics of some sort there. Why else would he be so anxious to get that crowd of armed men up onto that mountain? I deemed the situation potentially dangerous.

I sent cavalry to close off the roads and ordered the army to move against the mob. Many were killed and many taken captive. I directed that the leaders be executed.

The Samaritan Senate sent an embassy to Vitellius, who as President of Syria, was my superior. They accused me of murder. Vitellius ordered me to Rome to respond to their charges before Tiberius.

The final outcome was not so serious for me as it might have been earlier for a friend of Sejanus. Tiberius was smothered during my voyage to Rome, and Caligula was interested in other things. I was sent into exile and forgotten. My undoing was complete enough though not fatal. It was for me as it has been for so many other rulers of Palestine. The morass of religious problems engulfed me, despite my caution.

I spent my years there trying to subdue the rebellious spirit of the Jews. At the same time I had to avoid serious disorder because of the possibility of Parthian intervention, which would threaten the stability of the Near East. Always I kept in mind my responsibility to avoid embarrassing Sejanus and affecting the equilibrium of the entire world.

Ultimately I did not fail Sejanus. If I failed Rome it was because I left the same problems there when I departed that I found when I arrived. The same is true of Felix, Fadus, Albinus, Festus, and Florus, procurators who followed me, even though they have employed stronger measures than I did. Romans finally are coming to understand that, if the people of Palestine cannot be made to bend their stiff necks, we may have to break them.

I Am He

It had become the practice for the Governor to go up to Jerusalem during Passover Week, to see that order was preserved. The old city then was teeming with fervent pilgrims from throughout Judea and Galilee, and all the rest of the East as well. The danger of an outbreak of nationalistic disorder was greatest at such times. Accordingly, I was in residence at the royal palace built by Herod the Great during the last days of Jesus of Nazareth. Herod Antipas was also in the city for Passover. He stayed at the old Hasmonean palace near the Temple, which had been left to his family for use as a residence when they were visiting Jerusalem.

From my vantage point I followed the events of that Passover week with curiosity. At the time my own position, for the reasons I have given, was awkward, as is the situation with most public officials who have served any length of time; even though the causes vary with the individual and the circumstances.

My enemies in Palestine were many. I knew they

would do me whatever harm they could, whenever an opportunity presented itself. And in Rome, those men who were seeking to discredit Sejanus would magnify any embarrassment to his administration, at home or abroad.

After the arrest, Judas Iscariot was paid off and sent on his way. Jesus was taken to the palace of the High Priest.

It was just prior to that time that the Great Sanhedrin had been divested of its authority to impose the death penalty. Therefore, if, as a religious tribunal, it found a man guilty of heresy and worthy of death, it would have to ask the Governor to ratify the sentence before the man could be executed. The prescribed penalty was death by stoning, under the law of Moses. That is what they would have requested me to approve, if they had tried Jesus on a charge of heresy.

They had a number of reasons not to want to try him on that charge. He still enjoyed a great deal of support from the polyglot multitude of pilgrims who were in Jerusalem for Passover. If it developed that he had more public support than the chief priests of Judaism, the effect might be a serious one upon their faith.

They had other motives as well. The priestly hierarchy wanted the man disposed of quickly. There are several preliminary procedures which must be followed in Judea before a man may be put on trial as an apostate. These would have taken some days to get out of the way.

They took him prisoner on Thursday night. They wanted him executed the next day, before the sabbath. No executions are allowed on their holy days. The law of the Jews also provides that they could not judge on the eve of a sabbath or any other holy day. Furthermore, judgment could be rendered on the same day as the trial only if the verdict was for acquittal. If the guilty sentence was to be pronounced it could only be done on the day following the trial. Their law says, "He delays his judgment and lets it rest all night, that he may winnow out the truth." The following day would have been the sabbath, when the action of pronouncing sentence would have been forbidden anyway.

There were other complications relative to a formal trial for heresy. Jewish legal procedure requires that a heretical teacher must be questioned by two lower courts before being tried before the Great Sanhedrin. The authorities wanted to avoid these preliminary proceedings and thereby expedite the matter.

It would have been too many days before he could be formally tried as a heretic, dangerous days perhaps. Rather than waiting until the break of the second day of the week, as they were required to do before they could take any official action, a number of the members of the council convened in the night at the call of Caiaphas. They met in his palace to conduct a sort of irregular inquest. Their purpose was to interrogate the prisoner to establish him as an apostate, but they did not intend to present that charge against him to me. They wanted confirmation of their own conclusions that he was a false messiah. They also wanted to have proof to present to the Jewish people. By the way, I have no evidence that the Pharisees, with whom he had so often crossed swords, were involved in these proceedings against the man.

Instead of being heard before two lower courts, the carpenter was taken before Annas, the old man who was the patriarch of a whole family of High Priests. In his chambers Annas questioned Jesus about his doctrines. The Galilean answered that he had always taught in public and that Annas should ask those who had heard him in the temple. Having gained nothing to use against him, Annas sent him before those priests and elders who were by that time assembled in the palace of Caiaphas.

The High Priest himself presided at this meeting. Witnesses were called in against Jesus to testify that he had been quilty of blasphemy in his public statements. Jewish law requires that two witnesses be found who agree in their accusations and their accounts of events. The witnesses who appeared did not agree.

At last two men came who swore that the carpenter once said, "I will destroy this temple made with hands and within three days I will build another not made with hands."

Christians say he was speaking figuratively, referring to his own body when he used the term *temple*. They also maintain that the witnesses misrepresented what he actually did say and that he never asserted that he would destroy it himself.

If the allegations of the witnesses were to be accepted, and if the statements attributed to Jesus were to be taken literally, then he had made an undeniable assertion of his own divinity. But even the testimony of these two witnesses was inconsistent as to details, and would therefore have been inadmissible in a trial.

In the face of all of this the carpenter kept his peace, showing great dignity, I was told. The questions he had been asked and the charges made against him all related to apostasy. He must have known that they were not properly constituted to consider that charge, and did not choose to answer them.

If this proceeding had been a duly authorized trial for heresy by the Great Sanhedrin, he should have been declared not guilty and charges should have been pressed against the witnesses; but it was not such a trial.

Having failed up to this point to establish any guilt, Joseph ben Caiaphas stood up and walked forward to the defendant and said to him, "I adjure you by the living God that you tell us if you are the Christ, the son of God."

Then Jesus of Nazareth did what he had apparently come to Jerusalem to do. He said, "I am He."

That is an answer which cannot be fully appreciated by anyone who is not a Jew. The phrase "I am He" has mighty connotations, as I mentioned earlier. It appears often in their scriptures, but only in the mouth of their god himself. A typical quotation is: "I am He, and there is no other God beside me." Another example is: "I am He who blots out your transgressions for my sake."

The carpenter's choice of words was startling to his hearers because of what they considered to be the enormity of the impiety they conveyed. Jesus went on to stagger them further by saying, "And you shall see the Son of Man sitting on the right hand of power and coming in the clouds of heaven." This was a reference to a description written by their prophet Daniel of the coming of the messiah.

Then Caiaphas rent his robes, as he would have done at a trial for apostasy when pronouncing a guilty verdict. He cried out, "What need have we for witnesses? You have heard his blasphemy. What is your opinion?" All of the men who were gathered there agreed that he was worthy of death.

Jesus had been reported to have said earlier something to the effect that his life was not going to be taken from him, he was going to lay it down. That is what he did, instead of remaining silent as before.

There is a passage in a book of Jewish scripture called *The Wisdom of Solomon* that must have been in his mind that night. It ascribes these thoughts to wicked men:

"Let us therefore lie in wait for the just man, because he is not for our turn and he is contrary to our doings, and up-braideth us with transgressions of the law, and devulgeth against us the sins of our way of life. He boasteth that he hath knowledge of God, and calleth himself the Son of God . . . We are esteemed by him as triflers and he abstaineth from our ways as from filthiness, and he preferreth the latter end of the just, and glorieth that he hath God for a father. Let us see then if his words be true, and let us prove what shall happen to him, and we shall know what his end shall be. For if he be the true son of God, He will defend him, and will defend him from the hand of his enemies . . . Let us condemn him to a most shameful death, for there shall be respect had unto him by his words. These things they thought and were deceived, for they did not know God's hidden plan."

I say that this passage was in the mind of Jesus that night because he seemed to be aware of every scriptural reference that might be applied to himself, and he saw them as being fulfilled by the events in his life. The scholars who sat in judgment upon him that night may also have been thinking of that chapter of *The Wisdom of Solomon* and how Jesus must regard them, if he were the sincere victim of stupendous delusions that he seemed to be.

Jesus was held all night in the palace of Caiaphas until he could be brought before me in the morning.

When dawn came Judas Iscariot reappeared, acting quite distraught, having realized at last the effect of what he had done He tried to return the money to the chief priests and elders saying, "I have betrayed an innocent man." They refused to accept it. They said to him, "That is your problem, not ours. You look to it."

With a burden on his conscience he could not bear, he went out and hanged himself. He became the first of many to die on account of Jesus of Nazareth.

The Trial

Early Friday morning they brought the carpenter before me in the hall of judgment. The members of the council stayed outside, as well as the crowd that had come with them, because any Jew who entered a house or building which contained leavened bread at that season would be defiled and could not partake of the Passover feast.

The prisoner stood before me with his hands bound. Although he had been mistreated throughout the night, he still was very impressive. He was tall and strong. Tradition so described the messiah, and Jesus was never faulted on grounds of not looking as the messiah should, not even when he was being assailed for every other cause imaginable.

Like all Jews, he parted his hair in the middle and wore it falling to his shoulders, combed, and anointed with oil. Like all Jews, he wore a full beard and a mustache. He was dignified, apparently sustained by an unshaken faith in his god and himself.

The chief priests and elders stood outside the hall of judgment to present their accusations. I went out to them and asked, "What charges do you bring against this man?" The reports that I had received from inform-ants about their meeting at the palace of Caiaphas were still sketchy, but I was already aware their true complaint against him was that they held him to be a heretic.

They must have been aware that I knew. Someone replied, "We wouldn't have brought him to you if he weren't a criminal."

I said to them, "Take him and try him according to your laws." The Jewish law under which they might try him was their religious code. What I was telling them in effect was, "Try him for heresy, since that is the crime you wish to punish him for."

Someone else from among them replied, "It is not lawful for us to put any man to death," rather a mean-ingless non-sequitur. Under the new restrictions imposed upon them, they could and did find men guilty of apostasy, and they did stone them, although, as I ex-plained earlier, they had to obtain an approval of the death sentence from the Governor.

They were determined that they were not going to do that. They said, "We found this fellow perverting the nation, and forbidding Jews to give tribute to Caesar. He says that he himself is Christ, that he is a king."

There was in this accusation no word about the matters which had been discussed only hours before in the meeting at the palace of Caiaphas. The indictment was made on political grounds only. The defendant stood accused of instigating resistance to the laws and rule of Rome. The crime they accused him of was *laese maiestas*. They wanted me to try him, convict him, and execute him for them, on the pretext that he was an enemy of Caesar's.

It was quite unnatural for many of those men to be accusing any man of treason to Rome. Since Pompey's conquest, they had not ordinarily concerned themselves about revolutionaries. The majority of the members of the Sanhedrin had lost their lives for taking the part of Hezekiah against Herod the Great, years before, and their sympathy at that very time for a ruffian named Jesus Barabbas is a subject to which I shall allude shortly.

They wanted me to dispose of Jesus of Nazareth because then it would be done quickly, in a matter of a few hours; but I was not disposed to do it. Their convenience was not mine. I was not concerned about the carpenter's attacks on the Sadducees. His only real assault upon them had come when he drove the merchants out of the temple. That was a matter which could be resolved without too much damage to anyone.

I was not concerned about the man's attacks on the Pharisees either. Unlike the Sadducees, they had done nothing to enlist my sympathies during the four years since I had arrived. If, through bringing pressure to bear, he forced them to accept changes distasteful to them, it was no problem of mine. Besides, they didn't seem to be much involved that day, if at all.

As to the fear of revolt and destruction, I did not share it. The Galilean had had plenty of opportunities to give evidence of revolutionary attitudes, and had never done so. I was not apprehensive of an outbreak of rebellion if he were allowed to live a few more days while the proper procedures were followed by the men who had decided that he must die.

Some of them were also hoping to evade certain problems by having Jesus tried before me as governor. By so doing they would avoid bearing the onus of his death among his still substantial following. However, I did not care to incur an enmity they seemed to apprehend for themselves.

The essential reason that brought Jesus of Nazareth to stand fettered before me was that the chief priests and elders had concluded in an irregular hearing that he was guilty of apostasy. A colonial governor should resist all efforts to make him one of the spiders in a web of religious orthodoxy. I was determined not to let them enmesh me in it.

From his own actions, words, and predictions, it was evident that strange man had decided he was going to die on that day, but I was no more willing to be used by him as an instrument of self-destruction than I was employed as a weapon by the Jewish hierarchy.

I wished to refer the matter to the Sanhedrin, to be dealt with as an ecclesiastical case. The men outside the hall made a mistake in rejecting my proposal. For, if I tried him and found him guilty, he would be crucified rather than stoned. That would fulfill various prophecies about the way their god's great servant would die. Because of those same prophecies, Jesus had always predicted crucifixion for himself, which continued to seem improbable to me right down to the last day of his life.

Like the matter of the thirty pieces of silver, he could not make these prophecies come true, but his enemies could. Yet they seemed to be concerned only about the problems of that day. They insisted on accusing him of sedition, so he had to be tried on that complaint.

I said to him, "Are you the King of the Jews?"

He replied rather coolly, "Do you ask this question yourself, or did other men put it to you?"

I answered him, "Am I a Jew? Your own nation and chief priests have delivered you to me. What have you done?"

"My kingdom is not of this world," he said, as calmly

as if he had been Caesar speaking about the lands beyond the Rhine frontier. "If my kingdom were of this world, then my servants would have fought to keep me from being delivered to my enemies."

I remembered that his friends had been willing to fight in Gethsemane, but he had forbidden them, at a time when a skirmish in the darkness might have given him an opportunity to make good an escape. Therefore, the fact that he was before me confirmed that his reply reflected his actual beliefs. The warning against rebellion implied in his prophecy about the destruction of the Temple, his counsel to the Jews to render unto Caesar the things that are Caesar's, and his refusal to accept a crown on the shore of the Lake of Tiberias, all were in keeping with the answer he gave me, as were his admonitions to turn the other cheek, walk the extra mile, and so forth. It was clear to me that his monarchical claims were mystical, not political. It was evident that he was not guilty of treason as charged.

I recognized there still were problems for me in releasing him. After all, Caiaphas was my appointee and my ally. I counted upon his support. He was a faithful friend from the day I arrived in Judea till the day I sailed back to Rome.

Caiaphas was on the spot, therefore I was, too. I wanted to be well justified for my action of acquitting the carpenter, in order to minimize the temporary strain in our relationships that must result. So I pursued the line of questioning further.

I said to Jesus again, "You are a king then?"

He answered quietly, "It is as you say. To this end was I born, and for this cause was I brought into the world, that I should bear witness to the truth."

"What is the truth?" I said.

Caesar himself might have envied the prisoner standing there with his hands bound, straight and tall, for thinking he knew the truth, when the rulers of the world, the philosophers, and men of science concede they do not.

Such a magnificent assurance is often one enviable feature of madness. However, I would not have considered Jesus any more unbalanced than most, were it not for the fact that I knew he thought that his death was a necessary sacrifice to save mankind from its sins, that he would rise again from the dead, and that he was the only son of the Jewish god. During his appearance before me I became convinced that he believed those things. I have always been inclined to the view that his delusions were based upon the stories that Mary and Joseph told him when he was young. I suppose he would have been as normal as most of us, except for that.

It is said that, in a country where the majority is insane, they would lock up the people who are not. Jesus of Nazareth was so impressive and serene that I began to wonder if he was in fact the one who was mad, or if he was better off than the rest of us. At the very least it might be said that there were graceful threads of sanity running through the brilliant fabric of his dreams.

As these thoughts turned in my head, the chief priests shouted many accusations against him from outside, but he kept his peace. I said to him, "You hear how many things they say against you. Have you no answer?" He did not deign to reply.

I stepped down from the judgment seat and walked out to address the impatient crowd at the gates and said, "I find no fault in him at all."

That assorted mixture of dignitaries and rabble became more vehement. They shouted that he had been stirring up the Jews throughout Judea and Galilee.

That reference to Galilee suggested an idea. I asked

them if Jesus of Nazareth was a Galilean. This caused them to wonder. They knew that I could hardly be ignorant of the location of the city of Nazareth.

They had to answer that he was a Galilean. I pointed out in reply that he therefore belonged to the jurisdiction of Herod Antipas. I took the opportunity to deliver this troublesome matter to someone else, who would not be under pressure from the religious hierarchy in Jerusalem in the way I was. Herod did not have to live with them. Although the tetrarch was in Jerusalem for the Passover, with many of his subjects, he would soon be leaving for Galilee. He could afford to be objective.

I could not actually relinquish legal jurisdiction in the case to Herod Antipas, but I could submit the matter to him and perhaps gain the authority of his support for the decision I intended to render.

I expected that the tetrarch would not play the game of the priesthood in this affair. Herod was not likely to be interested in having government involved in the enforcement of religious discipline. I expected that he would see the case as I did, and exonerate the carpenter of the crime of treason. Herod might well have responded differently if the charge had been heresy, considered by the Great Sanhedrin under due process of law. I do not doubt that he would have been willing to accept the decision of the court.

Herod Antipas was a practical man and a good politician, which argued in favor of his concurring with me that, if the religious authorities wanted to execute the fellow for apostasy, they should try him on that charge, find him guilty, and receive routine permission from me to stone him.

I had another reason to send Jesus to the tetrarch. We had been at odds with each other for some time.

This was an opportunity to make a friendly gesture toward him that he would appreciate. Therefore, I sent the prisoner and his host of accusers to the old palace where Herod Antipas was staying. Herod was pleased, as I anticipated he would be.

It was a favor to him because he had been anxious to see the famous carpenter for a long time. He had heard a great deal about Jesus of Nazareth during the previous two or three years. In addition to all of the official reports he had received about the man, he had other sources of information. For example, the wife of his chief steward, a woman named Joanna, was among the most devoted followers of Jesus.

Herod had earlier been interested in John the Baptist, and had heard him willingly, until John began to hurl his thunderbolts in the direction of the tetrarch's wife. The ruler of Galilee was interested in Jesus because of his suspicion that he might be the reincarnation of John. His curiosity was aroused. All of the stories about the miracles of Jesus also intrigued him. Herod wanted to see a miracle, therefore he wanted to see Jesus.

The tetrarch did not know he had already seen him at various times in the past. Jesus must have recalled those occasions when, as a boy in Nazareth, he had seen his ruler passing by in splendid procession. Probably the carpenter's feelings in the face of all that pomp in the old Hasmonean palace were no more approving than they had been long before. The old prince, on the other hand, was disposed to be friendly and wanted to be entertained.

If the poor fellow standing in his bonds could have worked a miracle before his king, he could have saved himself. Perhaps I should say, if he *would* have rather than, if he *could* have. He certainly was capable of some unusual things, by all accounts. On that day he never wavered in his resolution to do nothing to save himself.

Herod questioned him at length, but the prisoner refused to make any reply, even while the chief priests and scribes stood around him making accusations. Throughout the episode he remained silent. His enemies among the Jews feel he was moved by the spirit of the devil to take actions which would appear to be the fulfillment of prophecies. The Jewish prophet Isaiah wrote concerning the messiah, "He was oppressed and he was afflicted, yet he opened not his mouth. He is brought as a lamb to the slaughter, and as a sheep before his shearers is dumb, so he openeth not his mouth."

Of course, the Christians do view his silence before Herod and me as prophecy fulfilled, and without doubt he did, too.

The priests and scribes who stood there accusing him were scholars and students of the Hebrew scriptures. They were highly offended by what he was doing, because they understood fully what he was up to.

As I anticipated, Herod Antipas thought Jesus of no political consequence, and judged that he had done nothing worthy of death. Yet the tetrarch and his retainers were annoyed by his impertinent silence, so they arrayed him in a gorgeous robe, to make light of his regal claims, as well as to show that Herod did not consider the matter to be a serious one. Then they sent him back to me.

I called together the chief priest and other rulers among the Jews and said, "You have brought this man before me, on the grounds that he has been perverting the people. I have examined him and found no fault in him with respect to the charges brought against him. Neither has Herod, who found nothing in him worthy of death. Therefore, I will chastise him and release him."

He had claimed to be a king and had therefore committed an offense. However, he had qualified the claim by saying his kingdom was not of this world. A penalty less than death should satisfy Roman law and be an appropriate response to those who accused him, since they had chosen to charge him only with treason.

I said to them, "You have a custom that I should release a prisoner to you at Passover. Shall I scourge and release the King of the Jews?"

I asked the question in the expectation that there would exist in any crowd in Jerusalem some remnant of the enthusiastic feeling for him that had been manifested only a few days before, when he entered the city. I was soon to be disillusioned. The men outside were not a cross-section of the people of Jerusalem. The general public was only slowly becoming aware of what was taking place. Word was circulating as the trial proceeded.

It was just as I sat down in the judgment seat to hear their reply and dispose of the matter that I received a message from my wife, saying, "Have nothing to do with that just man: I have suffered many things in a dream because of him."

For this act that good woman is considered by some Christians to be something of a saint; they believe she received a message from their god. I am glad she is remembered, even if it is by those strange people.

I was concerned by her premonition. Even though we no longer know what gods to believe in, or what doctrines to honor, everyone takes heed of dreams. What Roman does not remember the story of how Calpurnia, the night before Julius Caesar died, dreamed that her husband's image ran blood from a hundred wounds? We all live with the memory of the penalty Caesar paid for disregarding that warning.

While I was pondering the meaning of the message from my dear Claudia, the chief priests and elders were persuading the crowd outside to call for the release of a prisoner named Jesus Barabbas rather than Jesus of Nazareth.

I really did not want to let this Barabbas go. He was a man who had been involved in sedition and murder. As a leader of insurrection he was a hero to some Jews. There were some of his admirers among the crowd, men who had greeted the carpenter as their messiah on the first day of that same week. Having so fervently hailed Jesus as their savior a few days before, in the expectation that he was a miracle worker who would overthrow Roman rule, their fervor turned into repugnance upon seeing he was not. The rest of the crowd was made up of the chief priests and the elders, and their adherents. If there were those outside the gates who still believed that Jesus of Nazareth was the son of their god, I presume they were hoping he would deal with the situation himself, to the confusion of his adversaries. If he did so, there was no need for them to speak; if he didn't, they would be well advised to hold their tongues in that gathering.

I repeated my question to the crowd, "Which of the two shall I release, Barabbas, or Jesus who is called the Christ?"

They called out for Barabbas.

I asked, "What shall I do then with Jesus of Nazareth?"

They answered, "Crucify him!"

I asked them, "Why? What evil has he done?" Certainly he had done nothing of what he had been accused.

They gave no answer but to cry out, "Crucify him!"

Hoping to mollify their animosity for the poor fellow, I ordered him scourged. When this was done he was led away to the Praetorium by the soldiers, who were members of a Syrian legion who had no love for Jews. They plaited a crown of thorns and pressed it down upon his brow. They draped a purple robe over his shoulders and put a reed into his hands as a mock sceptre. Then they fell to their knees around him and pretended to worship him, crying, "Hail, King of the Jews!"

When it had gone far enough, I ordered them to bring him forth. I presented him to the hostile crowd with the words, "Behold the man." I hoped that pitiful figure would arouse their sympathy, and make them relent in their determination to destroy him. I thought they would surely see that he was not the threat that they had earlier believed him to be. However, he had so filled them with fear and horror, that they could not adjust to reality when that tragic-comic figure appeared before them with his mock crown and robe and his bloody brow and body.

It had no effect. In all my attempts at conciliation I succeeded only with Herod Antipas, whose enmity I turned into friendship on that day. I failed in my efforts to spare the prisoner and to satisfy the Jewish authorities with a punishment appropriate to the modest civil offence Jesus had committed.

It was all in vain. The priests, the scribes, the zealots, and all the rest of them cried out, "Crucify him!"

My patience was exhausted. I said, "You take him and crucify him. I find no fault in him."

I wished to be through with the whole affair. It is a pity it didn't end there and then. He could have left the hall of judgment, discredited as the messiah for whom the Jews were praying. Disgraced, he could have preached in the streets to smaller and smaller congregations as he grew older, and he could at last have been buried and forgotten.

He had come to Jerusalem to die and serve his own strange purposes by so doing, and they cooperated with him. Ultimately it appears that he knew what he was doing, and they didn't, with all their learning and wisdom.

They said to me, "We have a law, and by our law he ought to die, because he made himself the Son of God."

It was an error for them to state openly their true motivation for prosecuting him, because it did not relate to the charges they brought against him, nor to any crime under Roman law. However, I reflected on it in a way that surprised me.

The bearing of the man through all of his tribulations had been regal. He made me feel as though it was I who was on trial before him, a strange sensation.

I have always been a man of deliberate judgment. My wife's dream seemed to me an omen; I began to want to be careful of what I was doing.

I went back to the judgment hall and asked the quiet bloody figure standing there for his answer to the basic question he had raised with his claims. I said, "Where do you come from?"

He looked back at me calmly from under his spiked crown and gave me no answer. Now he had me thinking of those words from their prophet Isaiah, "He was oppressed and he was afflicted, yet he opened not his mouth."

In times past, I had had that whole passage translated for me, along with other scriptures relating to the messiah. Part of it went, "He was wounded for our transgressions, he was bruised for our iniquities . . . and with his stripes we are healed." The case was becoming disconcerting to me.

I said to him, "Why don't you answer me? Don't you realize that I have the power to crucify you? And that I have the power to release you?"

His self-possession was unshaken. He answered at last,

with a level look, "You could have no power over me at all, unless it were given to you from above. Therefore, those who delivered me to you have the greater sin."

His calm confidence was a bit heart-rending. I decided to release him with no further delay. The punishment he had undergone was adequate, and it was time to get on with other things. But the crowd assembled at the gates cried out, "If you let this man go you are no friend of Caesar's. Whoever tries to make himself a king sets himself up against Caesar."

It seemed ironic that the same men who called for the release of Barabbas would threaten me in this way. Yet I was disturbed by that cry. It cast a new and unpleasant light upon the matter. They had found a way to make the case of Jesus of Nazareth as much of a problem to me as it was to them.

Clearly the prisoner was not guilty of inciting rebellion as charged. Claiming a kingdom in another world is not a criminal offense under Roman law. However, he had indeed said he was a king, and a multitude had tried to crown him at the Lake of Tiberias after the affair of the loaves and fishes. And he had been accorded a triumphal entry into Jerusalem a few days before that would have done honor to Tiberius Caesar himself. Even though he had always advised his followers to obey Roman law, the Jewish authorities considered him a potential threat to the peace of the province. They continued to feel that such a man in Palestine might be made a political messiah by the force of circumstances, and that some mob might crown him yet. They could not dispel their fears that he might raise the flag of rebellion when it suited him. They had been alarmed by his bold challenges to their authority, and did not understand him as I did.

That cry from the crowd carried the threat that my

own enemies would accuse me of putting the peace of the province in jeopardy, if I let the man go. They could make a simple, convincing argument to support their case. Potential disorder in Palestine was a worry to Rome, what with the memory of Parthian intervention in the Jewish civil war there during the early years of Herod the Great. No one doubted that the Parthians would seize any opportunity that was presented to extend their power. No one wanted another war between Parthia and Rome at that time, except the Parthians perhaps. Rome desired status quo, as usual.

It might be hard for me to convince Rome that the carpenter not only was not a danger to the established order of government but that he never would be. If the enemies of Sejanus could claim that my administration in Palestine had created a risk to the peace of the East, the debate would not help my benefactor and protector, nor would it help Rome.

In those days, Sejanus seemed to rule the world like a god. Yet such a man at the peak of his power is on a precarious height, and his footing can be treacherous. He can fall to his ruin all too easily. My obligations to myself and my friend would not allow me to incur even a minimal risk for the life of one itinerant street preacher. Always I had to play clearly the role of guardian of Roman rule and Caesar's interests.

Even though I knew that poor visionary of a carpenter was no threat to the government, I concluded that releasing him could be. My choice was made for me by the determined men at the gate. He was more important to them than he was to me.

At the moment I resented being manipulated by them into condemning an innocent man I had begun to admire in an odd way. I took no pains to conceal my feelings from them. I brought Jesus forth and sat down in my judgment seat to pronounce the sentence. I taunted the men at the gate by saying to them, "Behold your king!"

They shouted, "Away with him! Crucify him!"

I answered, "What? Shall I crucify your king?"

They cried, "We have no king but Caesar," and there was great tumult among them.

The Jews have a ceremony they perform when the body of a man who has been murdered is found, and the killer cannot be identified. The elders of the town say an ancient prayer, "Be merciful, O Lord, unto thy people Israel, whom thou hast redeemed, and lay not innocent blood to them." Then they wash their hands ceremonially in public.

To show them what I thought of the whole business, I sent for a basin of water and washed my hands before them, saying, "I am innocent of the blood of this just man. Look you to it."

My reference to a ritual which is used in cases of murder antagonized the crowd. One of them shouted, "May his blood be on us, and on our children!" Some others took up the angry cry. Unfortunately, that awful phrase was recorded by Christians in their writings, otherwise I would not mention it. If Christianity should persist, I am afraid it may be a cause of grief for a lot of innocent people.

At the third hour of the day I sent Jesus of Nazareth out with a centurion and a small guard to be crucified.

The Crucifixion and What Followed

They took him to a little knoll outside the city wall called Calvary, the place of the skull, to crucify him there between two thieves. He had been so weakened by the scourging that he couldn't carry his cross as the law provides. The centurion had to press a bystander into service to bear it for him. At Calvary, after the nails had been driven through his hands and feet, and the cross had been dropped into its hole, he said, "Father, forgive them." Then he added, "They know not what they do." Those who had arranged his death, the men for whom he prayed, little knew how truly he spoke, though they would soon learn.

The centurion in charge of the executions asked me to specify the crime for which he was being punished, in order that it might be posted upon the cross, according to the usual procedure. By that time I was not disposed to cater to the sensitivities of the religious establishment any further. I wrote, "Jesus of Nazareth, King of the

Jews," and ordered it to be nailed to the cross over his head, in Latin, Greek, and Aramaic.

The chief priests objected. They said, "Do not say 'King of the Jews,' write, 'He said, I am King of the Jews.'"

I answered, "What I have written, I have written."

In the course of the hours, as he was dying what Cicero correctly called the most cruel and hideous of deaths, there were the usual sad scenes. Some of the priests and scribes there stood about and chided him, saying among other things, "Let Christ the King of Israel now descend from the cross." They did it to discredit him by public ridicule, to render more unlikely the possibility of a heretical cult arising around his memory. They were conscious of the danger even then. Probably some of them also stayed until the end for his sake in the hope that he would confess his error to them in the face of death. Confession of sin and repentance are important in their religion and they may have wanted to relieve his soul of some of its burden before it left his body.

More casual and cruel were the taunts of the Syrian legionaries there, which echoed those of the priests. The soldiers like to find an outlet for their hostility to the Jews. Usually their only diversions were to be found in bad women, worse wine, and endless games of horseshoes. They welcomed any occasion to break the monotony.

His mother was there watching her hopes perish before her eyes. There was a considerable number of people who followed him grief-stricken to Calvary. They stayed until he died. The priests and scribes there must have taken some grim satisfaction from the fact that his popularity among Jews even at such time confirmed the correctness of their decision that it was necessary to save some of their people from themselves in this way.

With the passing of the hours some unusual things took place that caused his departure from this life to be as peculiar as his entry into it had been.

The first of them stemmed from the fact that he had a cloak which had been woven from top to bottom without a seam. When they stripped the carpenter and nailed him to the cross, the four soldiers divided each of his garments into four parts among them, but they did not want to tear his cloak, so they cast lots for it.

This was another of the odd coincidences which ultimately gave strength to Christianity, because David, the ancient Jewish king, wrote this passage concerning the man of god: "They parted my raiment among them and for my vesture did they cast lots."

It was never clear to me whether the priest and scribes picked up the significance of this occurrence that afternoon and its potential impact upon the future. Certainly Jesus did; he pointed it out in his dying minutes, when he began to repeat the psalm in which the passage occurs.

At the ninth hour of the day the naked man on the cross cried out, "My God, my God, why has thou forsaken me."

A casual hearer of the account of his death might assume that apparent cry of anguish would put an end to anyone's taking the man's claims seriously. If the poor fellow in that terrible hour, overwhelmed by the awful reality of his pain, expressed his own doubts in that sad cry, how could anyone else believe in him subsequently? The answer is that it was not a simple cry of anguish. "My God, my God, why hast thou forsaken me?" is the opening verse of a psalm of praise written by King David. It is that psalm which contains the lines, "They parted my garments among them and cast lots upon my vesture." In it the psalmist also referred to the man of god in these words: ". . . the assembly of the wicked have enclosed me, they pierced my hands and my feet . . . and all my bones are out of joint . . ."

His cry was a reaffirmation of his claim that he was the messiah. It was also a restatement of his faith, and a last shout of praise for his god, as he hung there dying in agony.

The concluding verses of that psalm include these lines: "All the ends of the world shall remember and turn to the Lord: and all kindred of all nations shall worship before Thee.

"For the kingdom is the Lord's; and He is the governor of all nations."

Just as Jesus of Nazareth had been up until this hour unshaken in his faith, so he remained. He was dying with an assurance that any Roman would admire in a man, mad or sane.

During that afternoon there chanced to occur an extraordinary phenomenon. At the sixth hour of the day the sky darkened, as though betokening a sign from some supernatural power, and it remained dark until the ninth hour. This was disturbing to many.

Thallus the Samaritan, a distinguished historian in most respects, recently proposed that the darkness at the time of the death of Jesus must have been the eclipse of thirty years ago. It was not. These events took place three years before the eclipse. The lowering of the sky was some sort of atmospheric manifestation.

There are a great many earthquakes in Palestine. As mischance would have it, an earthquake was added to the darkening of the sky. That further alarmed the superstitious. The centurion at Calvary became afraid and showed it, saying, "Truly this was the son of god." These two coincidental occurrences, combined with the soldiers casting lots for Jesus' robe, proved to be as fortuitous for the growth of Christianity in the course of time as the coincidence surrounding his birth. Ultimately it was the events he and his followers could not arrange that illuminated the legend that surrounds his name.

The earthquake was another incident made pregnant with meaning by the scriptures of the Jews. The Christians are fond of quoting the following ancient passage in connection with the death of Jesus: "In my distress I called upon the Lord, and cried unto my God: He heard my voice out of his Temple, and my cry came before Him, even unto His ears. Then the earth shook and trembled; the foundations of the hills moved and were shaken."

Later that afternoon word spread that the earthquake had rent the veil that hung before the most holy place in the Temple. This, too, has been given great symbolic meaning by the Christians. They say it implied that the death of Jesus opened the way to their god.

The last words of Jesus of Nazareth were: "Father, into your hands I commend my spirit." Having uttered them, he bowed his head and gave up the ghost.

The Jewish authorities did not want to have the three men hanging naked on their crosses on the sabbath. They asked me to order that the men's legs be broken, in order that they would die quickly. It throws all of the crucified man's weight on his arms and makes his breathing more and more difficult, until he can breathe no more. I gave the command that it be done. However, the carpenter was already dead, which surprised me when I heard it, so his legs were not broken. Out of malice, one of the Syrian soldiers thrust his spear into his side, leaving no question about his death.

Jesus of Nazareth had accomplished what he had come to Jerusalem to do. The commentary of the astrologers about the star, the stories of Mary and Joseph about the angels, and the remark of John the Baptist about his being a lamb who was to die to take away the sins of the world had brought him to this ignominious end.

Almost the last thing he said was, "It is finished." It must have been a great relief to him to say it.

To hear him say it must also have been a great relief to the priests and scribes among the Jews there at Calvary. I am sure they said to themselves "Thank God!"

But it wasn't finished. It was only beginning.

A member of the Great Sanhedrin named Joseph of Arimathea, who had not taken part in the decision to prosecute Jesus, came and asked me for the body. If he had not done so, it would have been cast into the pit where the bodies of criminals were discarded with other refuse.

Joseph was a man of good reputation and considerable wealth. He was showing no little courage in making his request. It implied that he was a follower of Jesus, which was risky. The Great Sanhedrin had excommunicated the man who said he had been cured of blindness by Jesus because he insisted that the Galilean was a man of god.

At the time I didn't see what harm it could do, so I gave orders that the soldiers deliver the body to Joseph. That decision turned out to be an unfortunate one. However, I should like to point out that the consequences were not of the sort that even the most prudent man could have foreseen.

Joseph gave the carpenter a decent burial in his own new tomb which had been hewn into the rock in a garden adjacent to the place of execution. He caused a great stone to be rolled across the door of the sepulchre to protect it from intruders.

In the morning the chief priests and some others were before me again. They said to me, "Sir, we remember that the deceiver said, while he was still alive, 'After three days I will rise again,' therefore we request that you command that the sepulchre be made secure until the third day. Otherwise his disciples may come by night and steal him away, and say that he is risen from the dead. If that should happen, the situation will be more serious than before."

I made an additional mistake when I told them, "You have your own watch. They can provide security. You see to it."

So they went away and posted their own guard to protect the tomb from meddlers. They also sealed the great stone in its place across the entrance.

The next episode is the most important in the whole affair. On the morning of the following day the stone was found to have been rolled away. The tomb was empty, and the world was changed, though we didn't know it at the time.

The watch which had been posted to guard the tomb reported to the high priests that the disciples of Jesus had come in the night and had stolen the body while they were asleep. Then I regretted that I had not ordered a squad of Roman soldiers to stand watch. They would never have gone to sleep while on guard, not if they valued their skins.

The report of the watch is the explanation of the event accepted by the majority of the Jews today. The Christians maintain that the watch was bribed by the chief priests to say what they did. The positions each side takes is exactly what would be expected.

The Christians say that he rose again, as he promised he would. Some of his disciples claimed to have seen him in various places in Judea and Galilee during the next few weeks. Forty days after his resurrection, they say, he was caught up into heaven from the Mount of Olives. They say it happened not far from the place where he had been received in triumph by the multitude on the first day of Passover week.

There are a few who try to explain things by suggesting that he did not die on the cross at all. They propose that he was drugged by his friends into the appearance of death, or that he fell into a faint as a result of the pain he was suffering and returned to his senses in the tomb. They submit that he left the country, for the good of his cause, after an appropriate number of seemingly miraculous appearances.

That is a foolish proposition. There should be no doubt entertained but that he died. That Syrian soldier made sure of it with his spear. It never occurred to his enemies to think that he might have survived. They saw him die.

In any case, the question is purely an academic one. No one but his followers claimed to have seen the risen Jesus. Those who do not believe them don't trouble themselves with the question.

I realized the potential implications of the story of the empty tomb and made a report in full of the matter directly to Tiberius Caesar.

That was my last official act relating to Jesus of Nazareth.

Reflections

When I am reminded now of that poor deluded carpenter from Southern Galilee, and when I reflect upon his fate, I appreciate the comment of the poet Lucretius, "Religion has persuaded man to so many evils."

My own duty was to administer Roman justice. The aim of justice is inflexible; it is to protect the interests of the state and the public. If a government is to preserve anything at all, it must take care first to preserve itself.

In any case the death of Jesus was inevitable. He had predicted any number of times that he would die on the cross. Finally he announced that his time had come. Resigned to his own prophecies, he would take no steps to save himself. It is hard to save a man who doesn't wish to save himself. Especially a poor man.

As for the chief priests and elders among the Jews, the men upon whom I depended for support, they were rich and powerful. He had challenged them in ways they could not ignore without risking changes in their daily affairs and their religious doctrines. They felt that the doctrinal changes would cause their god to abandon their nation to spiritual destruction. They also harbored a real fear that he might eventually raise a rebellion and bring down a more prosaic ruin upon them. They took their responsibilities seriously and did what they decided they had to do. Their intentions were at least as good as those of most other public officials. In the time of Julius Caesar, the purest man in Rome was Brutus. His memory reminds us that aggressively virtuous men can be as great a danger to themselves and their own causes as they are to others.

To be fair, it must be remembered that the hierarchy of no religion will allow a man to live who claims to be a god of that faith, unless he can be set aside as a lunatic. Most other societies will simply ridicule such a man; but Judaism in this day and age is different. It holds that some fellow making the claim to be the savior of mankind and the son of god will be telling the truth. For the last century such fellows have not been laughed at in Jerusalem as they would be in Rome or Athens. Furthermore, the religious authorities decided that the miracles of Jesus were genuine, so they couldn't dismiss him as a mad man.

There was no doubt in my mind when the carpenter appeared before me that they would dispose of him by one means or another. While I resisted their plan to have me do the job for them, I did not doubt that they would find a way to kill him. Like a lot of very righteous men their intentions were better than their judgment. Their mistake was that, by securing his death upon the cross, they arranged for the fulfillment of his own prophecies and those of King David, thereby enhancing his credibility as the messiah.

They should not have prosecuted him for a crime of which he was innocent. Like so many other idealists in emergencies, they adopted the position that the end justifies the means. They did not achieve their end. Men seldom do, because there is no end to anything we do. Generally the means we employ are all that we are remembered for, and are the only ends after all.

In the course of describing the rush to Calvary, I mentioned that I came to feel that it was I who was on trial rather than he. That is how I presume the judges of Socrates must have felt centuries ago. Sometimes I have wondered if I am to go down in the memories of some men (if any Christians survive the current campaign of extermination) with the men who judged Socrates. It is an interesting thought to me, because, as a boy at my studies, I was troubled by the injustice of the execution of that gentle philosopher.

There are a number of parallels between the two men, and between the two trials as well.

Like Socrates, Jesus asked basic questions about customs and institutions, and challenged the religious establishment. Both of them believed in the immortality of the soul of man. Both held that there is only one god, who is the wise and just ruler of the world. Both were faithful in worship and prayer.

The Greek philosopher and the Galilean mystic were both effective in debate in public places in the capital city. By being profound as well as clever, they embarrassed the representatives of authority time after time.

Both were virtuous. Criticism is easier for important men to accept when it comes from men who are not too pure. Both were popular with the people. Both were poor.

Both Socrates and Jesus had the option to live and rejected it. Each had the alternative choice of exile. It was offered to Socrates by the rulers of Athens, and refused. It was no less available to Jesus, who could have gone to Galilee or Babylon or Egypt, or any of a hundred other places where Jews live outside the jurisdiction of the Great Sanhedrin. Instead, he went to Jerusalem and stayed there until the tragedy was played out.

Socrates maintained that he had a mission which was the duty to search for the truth and lead men to it. He viewed himself as an envoy of his god, just as Jesus did. The two of them said many of the same things about their gods. It is hard to tell some of the sayings of the young Jew from those of the old Greek.

There is one apparent difference. The real reason the Athenian government decided to silence Socrates was that his political opinions offended them .However, they prosecuted him on religious grounds. Jesus Christ was executed because the Jewish authorities decided he was guilty of religious offenses, but they prosecuted him for alleged political crimes. Yet I think that the fact that the two cases are so precisely opposite in this respect constitutes a further parallel rather than a difference between them.

The common truth is that people are willing to respect a man of principle only so long as he does not get in their way.

When prominent men are killed, it is almost always for much the same reasons. Was Julius Caesar murdered for being a great and noble man? Was Caligula assassinated for his madness and depravity? No. These peculiarities were forgiven them. Like Socrates and Jesus of Nazareth, both died for proposing to alter the existing order of things. Men qualify for assassination by becoming popular enough or powerful enough to pose a threat to status quo.

If a man in public life is willing to accept things as

they are, he will avoid being loved or hated, and his death will be as peaceful as his life.

I began this chapter with a reference to the comment of Lucretius that "Religion has persuaded man to so many evils." It is true simply because there are always elements trying to distort every religion and institution. The Christians are as vulnerable as everyone else. I have heard that some of the gentiles among them are already hating any Jews who do not convert, holding them responsible for the death of Christ. It makes about as much sense as blaming Greeks in general because the rulers of Athens arranged the judicial murder of Socrates. If there are people consumed by such curious malice, the thought of how they could ever consider themselves to be followers of Jesus of Nazareth is more than I can fathom.

Conclusion

Just seven weeks after the execution of Jesus of Nazareth I heard that the disciple called Peter preached to a multitude in Jerusalem at the Jewish Feast of Pentecost winning three thousand converts to the view that the crucified man was the messiah. The fact that so many Jews were willing to follow the carpenter even in death alarmed Annas and Caiaphas as much as anything the man had ever done in life, and rightly so. The day of Pentecost turned out to be a portent of what was to come. Ever since then Christianity has been spreading until now it has become a concern of the men who are charged with the welfare of the world. It ceased being simply a new Jewish sect and came to be a problem of general concern when the disciple named Paul got the other apostles of Jesus to agree that a person could become a Christian without first becoming a Jew.

Since then, the growth of Christianity has astonished everyone. The disciples who carried on the work of the carpenter were, for the most part, common laborers with no apparent qualifications to the religious leaders. Yet they preached their dead master's message with amazing effectiveness.

These ignorant fellows have been believed by multitudes when they said their god had sent them to preach that Jesus Christ is lord and judge of us all. Their authority was joyfully accepted when they proclaimed that he was the first-born among mankind to rise from death to immortality, and when they said that anyone who chose to could follow him, when their time came to die.

His disciples were soon reported to me to be working miracles in his name, healing the sick and casting out devils. The Christians say that both Peter and Paul resurrected dead men into life. I began to hear of disturbances wherever they went. Before long Jews were bringing their sick out into the streets in the hope that Peter's shadow would fall upon them as he passed.

The Jewish authorities were soon expressing their concerns to me again. The devotion of the new converts to Christianity was total. Members of the burgeoning cult gave away all of their possessions and had all things in common. This was one feature of the new religion that made respectable people feel uneasy about it, along with the stories about their drinking blood. Another factor which has subsequently aroused the same response, in Italy, is that generally the Christians are slaves and poor people, the dirty, the disorderly, and the vulgar.

Actually the popularity of Christianity among the lower classes is not surprising. It gives them a hope of bliss in the next world. They have never before been encouraged to expect happiness anywhere.

Due to recent prosecutions, Christianity has become a sort of secret society, using a simple line drawing of a fish as its symbol. This sign was chosen because *ichtheus*, the Greek word for *fish*, is made up of the first letters of the Greek words for *Jesus Christ, Son of God, Savior*. This is the reason they are coming to be known as the people of the fish.

The Jewish hierarchy, having set their hands to the plow with the crucifixion of Jesus, continued to try to uproot his influence from the soil of their land. They treated people who professed the new faith as heretics, even though the Christians at the beginning insisted that they were good Jews and wanted to be accepted as such. The first to be executed was a leader of the Greek faction of the church in Jerusalem named Stephen. The Sanhedrin tried him and ordered him stoned as an apostate.

When Herod Agrippa became King of the Jews he concerned himself with religious matters. At the beginning of his reign he was concentrating on a ticklish business, that of trying to deter Caligula from his plan to erect a gigantic statue of himself in the temple in Jerusalem and to require the Jews to worship him as a god.

Total destruction for Agrippa, the Jews, and the Christians, too, for that matter, was narrowly averted when the tribune of the Praetorian Guard sent Caligula to be with the other gods. The accession to the throne of the gentle Claudius came only just in time to save them all from annihilation. Later, Agrippa, who was a very orthodox Jew, also found time to try to discourage Christianity. He was stricken dead in Caesarea after reigning only three years, and the Christians broadcast their opinion that he was the object of divine retribution, for trying to thwart their god's will.

One by one the leaders of the cult have been eliminated. Herod Agrippa executed the one called James the Greater as part of his program of suppression of heresy.

James the Less, who emerged as the head of the

mother church in Jerusalem, was found guilty of apostasy by the Great Sanhedrin and stoned just two years ago. He died with the words of Jesus on his lips. "Father, forgive them, for they know not what they do."

After Agrippina fed Claudius his famous supper of toadstools, in order to put her son on the Imperial throne in the place of her husband, things took a turn for the worse for the people of the fish throughout the Empire. Under Nero the Christian leaders have lived courageously under the constant threat of death, and they have died with dignity. Their serene faith has unfortunately led their followers to walk in their footsteps.

Some rabbinic scholars sought other means of discouraging Jews from accepting Jesus of Nazareth as the Christ. To all of the arguments that had been used to try to discredit the carpenter during his lifetime, his adversaries added a new one after his death.

They cited certain provisions in the Jewish law relative to him. One clause states that an illegitimate child (their word is *momser*) is peculiarly inclined to apostasy. Because it is a disgrace to a Jew to be illegitimate, the circumstances of the birth of a momser are not to be referred to as long as he leads a righteous life. However, when any man has been adjudged to be an apostate, the fact that he is a momser should be made public, in order to discredit him with the people.

That has been done. The fact that Mary and Joseph were not married at the time Jesus was conceived has been made known to every Jew. His detractors claim to have identified his father as a Roman legionary named Panthera. Some members of the Jewish religious orders have taken to referring to him as Jesus ben Panthera. In the face of ridicule, hatred, and the impending death, Christians cling obstinately to their belief that their dead leader is the son of the Jewish god.

However, the word in general remains skeptical of the idea that gods still beget children of women in this day and age, as we are told they did in ancient times. Eons have passed since Jupiter sired Hercules and Perseus. It was at the very dawn of the world that Apollo became the father of Aesculapius.

From the time I first heard the miraculous stories about Jesus Christ, I concluded that they could only be true if he were in fact the son of a god. Who else would be born of a virgin and walk upon water? But naturally I had to dismiss such fanciful ideas. I was expected to be pragmatic in dealing with the problems of office. A high degree of probability has to be a sufficient test of truth for the premises upon which government bases its decisions.

Thirty years later and two thousand miles away, I can afford to assume a philosophical objectivity and consider the most unlikely possibilities. Even though it thoroughly mystifies most reasonable men that there are so many people who believe that poor carpenter was the son of the one true god, I think I must address myself to the subject. Having discussed everything else about Jesus of Nazareth, I should not lay down my pen before I dispose of the great claim he made for himself, which is the cornerstone of Christianity. And, after all, an intelligent man must be willing to consider anything to be possible until it has been proven otherwise.

With that rule in mind, I should like to refer to the counsel of the President of the Great Sanhedrin who spoke words of wisdom on the subject when almost everyone else was overwrought with emotion. He was a man named Gamaliel, a leader of the Pharisees, a doctor of the law, and either a son or grandson, I understand, of Hillel, the most honored Jewish teacher of modern times. The occasion was the trial before the Sanhedrin, of Peter and some of the others, who had been ordered not to teach in the name of Jesus but had continued to do so.

During the trial Gamaliel said to the members of the court, "You men of Israel, be careful of what you intend to do to these men.

"In times past there rose up Theudas, who claimed to be somebody, and hundreds of men joined him. He was slain and all who followed him were scattered, and it all came to nothing. After him there rose up Judas of Galilee in the days of the taxing, and he drew many people after him. He also perished, and all who followed him were dispersed.

"So I say to you, leave these men alone. If this counsel or this work be of men, it will come to nothing; but if it be of God, you cannot overthrow it."

These words of Gamaliel are the best guide for the rest of us as well.

It seems improbable that the new faith will survive the determination of Caesar to obliterate it. If the Emperor does succeed, the counsel of Gamaliel will give us the answer that Jesus of Nazareth was a poor mad fellow who misled himself and others into a tragic error.

However, if it transpires with the passage of time that the church in Rome survives, if the time comes when there are as many men who believe that Jesus of Nazareth is the son of a god as there are who believe Hercules is, and if it ever comes to pass that there are as many people who pray for healing in the name of Christ as there are who pray in the name of Aesculapius, when all of these unlikely things take place, and not before, it will be time to draw from the wisdom of Gamaliel another conclusion about Jesus, Mary, the angels, and all the rest.